D1027957

MATTHEW ARNONE • MATTHEW ARNONE •

Decades of our Lives

2000s

Decades of our Lives

CLASSIC, RARE, AND UNSEEN

2000s

FROM THE ARCHIVES OF THE DAILY MAIL

Trans
Atlantic
Press

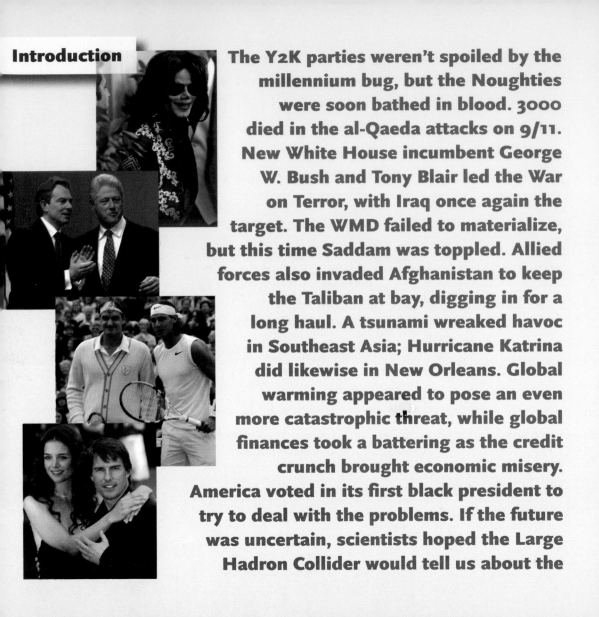

The Y2K parties weren't spoiled by the millennium bug, but the Noughties were soon bathed in blood. 3000 died in the al-Qaeda attacks on 9/11. New White House incumbent George W. Bush and Tony Blair led the War on Terror, with Iraq once again the target. The WMD failed to materialize, but this time Saddam was toppled. Allied forces also invaded Afghanistan to keep the Taliban at bay, digging in for a long haul. A tsunami wreaked havoc in Southeast Asia; Hurricane Katrina did likewise in New Orleans. Global warming appeared to pose an even more catastrophic threat, while global finances took a battering as the credit crunch brought economic misery. America voted in its first black president to try to deal with the problems. If the future was uncertain, scientists hoped the Large Hadron Collider would tell us about the past by recreating Big-Bang conditions. Most kids were more interested in social networking sites. Reality TV dominated the schedules, and anyone could become a star on YouTube. *The Deathly Hallows* marked the final outing for publishing phenomenon Harry Potter. Usain Bolt and Michael Phelps were the fastest things on land and water at the Beijing Olympics; Jonny Wilkinson's boot won the Rugby World Cup for England; Zidane was the best footballer on the planet but saw red in the 2006 World Cup final. Federer ended Sampras's Wimbledon reign, and went on to overtake his Grand Slam haul. From the momentous and the apocalyptic to the offbeat and the trivial, the photographs in this book, from the archives of the *Daily Mail*, chart the people, places, and events that made up a memorable decade.

2000

RIGHT: London's stunning Millennium footbridge under construction. The pedestrian-only steel suspension bridge designed by Norman Foster was planned to link the City and St Paul's Cathedral on the north bank of the River Thames with the Tate Modern on the south. The bridge was officially opened by the Queen on June 10, 2000 but closed after a few days when pedestrians found the structure was wobbling. Modifications were made and it again opened two years later.

OPPOSITE: Trapeze artists and acrobats entrance the audience in the heart of the Millennium Dome. With music composed by Peter Gabriel the show featured breath-taking acts using bungee stilts and sail diver rigs. Over the millennium year 999 performances were delivered with up to 12,000 people watching on each occasion. The Millennium Dome, designed by Sir Richard Rogers, was built to house the Millennium Experience an important exhibition to welcome in the next century. At the end of the year it closed and became home to a number of temporary events until it was reopened as the O2 concert arena in 2007 with Bon Jovi performing the first show.

ABOVE: Joaquin Phoenix and Russell Crowe confront each other in a scene from *Gladiator*. The American/ British epic directed by Ridley Scott also starred Derek Jacobi and Richard Harris. Oliver Reed, who played the role of a gladiator trainer died unexpectedly during filming so a digital body double was created to complete the final scenes and the film was dedicated to his memory. It received five Academy Awards, including one for Russell Crowe for Best Actor, four BAFTA Awards, and two Golden Globe Awards.

OPPOSITE: Tom Hanks is stranded on a desert island in the movie *Cast Away*. Directed by Robert Zemeckis, the movie unfolds the story of Hanks, a FedEx employee whose plane crashes on a South Pacific island; he then has to fight for survival using the contents of the parcels on the flight. It was a huge box-office success, and Hanks was nominated for an Academy Award as well as winning a BAFTA Award for Best Actor in a Leading Role.

ABOVE: A Muslim girl walks past fundamentalist graffiti in Nigeria in March 2000. A Muslim majority in the north and Christians living in the south of the country, combined with many inherent ethnic differences meant tensions were never far from the surface and Nigeria had a history of sectarian violence. In January, these troubles were further exacerbated when the state of Zamfara in the north introduced Sharia, or Islamic law against the wishes of the Christian population, who believed it restricted their freedom and way of life.

OPPOSITE: Burned-out vehicles litter the parking lot of the Apostolic Church in Kaduna, Nigeria, after an attack by Muslim rioters.

Israeli soldiers look on as Palestinians pray within the walls of Jerusalem. In July 2000 US President Bill Clinton convened a peace summit between Palestinian President Yasser Arafat and Israeli Prime Minister Ehud Barak. The summit began on July 11, 2000 and ended on July 25, without an agreement being reached. Each side blamed the other for the failure of the talks, the Palestinians claiming they were not offered enough, and the Israelis claiming that they could not reasonably offer more. In the months following the summit, Clinton appointed former US Senator George J. Mitchell to lead a fact-finding committee that later published the Mitchell Report.

Russian President Vladimir Putin surrounded by his entourage. After Boris Yeltsin's surprise resignation at the end of 1999, Putin was elected to the presidency and subsequently re-elected for a second term of office in 2004. He has always been a popular leader among Russians, bringing political stability, improving the economy, and reducing poverty. Owing to the country's constitution he was unable to stand again in 2008 but new President Dmitry Medvedev immediately nominated him for the post of Prime Minister.

2000

ABOVE: Nuno Gomes of Portugal scores the winning goal against England in the Euro 2000 competition. England were knocked out in the first round while Portugal stormed through the initial stages but were eventually beaten by France in the semi-finals. France went on to win the tournament, defeating Italy 1–0 in the final.

OPPOSITE: Thierry Henry rehearses for his part in an Arsenal charity pop video. The French striker had joined the Gunners in 1999 for £10.5 million and, under the wing of Arsène Wenger, he became the club's highest-scoring player, with a total of 226 goals. Henry was promoted to captain in his last two seasons with the club and led them to the final of the 2006 Champions League, where they lost by a narrow margin to Barcelona—the club which Henry joined the following year. Henry had similar success with his national side; he was part of the squad that won the 1998 World Cup and currently holds the record as France's top goalscorer.

2000

OPPOSITE: An aerial view of Pinewood Studios in Buckinghamshire, England, showing sets for the films *Mummy 2* and *Hornblower*. The studio, which has 41 stages, vast areas of land for shooting outdoor scenes, a huge water tank, and an underwater stage, has always been the home of the James Bond films.

RIGHT: Cousins Donjeta and Altina Hoxhaj stand in the charred remains of what was once their classroom in the hillside village of Vllazrimi-Crmjan in Western Kosovo. The school, serving five villages, was destroyed by paramilitaries as the families of Kosovo Albanians joined the exodus of more than 700,000 people into the refugee camps in neighboring Macedonia and Albania. Despite the scars of brutal ethnic cleansing and intense fighting between the KLA and Serb forces, help and healing came from international aid.

2000

ABOVE: Sasha Baron Cohen in the guise of his fictional character Ali G. Cohen had originally developed the character on Channel 4's *Eleven O' Clock Show*, interviewing several celebrities including David Beckham, Donald Trump, and Buzz Aldrin as Ali G. Through his spoof personality he was frequently able to embarrass interviewees or lead them to agree with inaccurate statements. Cohen later used him in the satirical television series *Da Ali G Show* along with new characters Borat and Brüno.

OPPOSITE: Jonathan Ross, the flamboyant British radio and television presenter, with his wife Jane and son Harvey. Ross started working with the BBC in 1997 presenting the film program and later began his Saturday morning radio show on BBC Radio 2. In 2001 the chat show *Friday Night with Jonathan Ross* was launched and although it attracted large audiences, Ross has been criticized because of his frequent inappropriate remarks. Awarded an OBE in 2005, he has often hosted events such as the Live 8 concerts, Live Earth, and Comic Relief.

LEFT: Britain's only black stunt-woman, Amanda Foster, bursts through a glass door during filming. In demand as a body double and stunt-woman, Foster stepped in for Whoopi Goldberg in *A Knight in Camelot* and had parts in many film and TV productions during the Noughties, including Bond movie *Die Another Day* and four of the Harry Potter films. Her impressive qualifications included precision truck driving, fencing skills, hang gliding, and Kung fu.

OPPOSITE: Music by Jan Garbarek and a dramatic laser show heralded the opening of the new Tate Modern gallery on the South Bank, London. Built inside the original Bankside Power Station, it was designed to house modern and contemporary art dating from 1900. The famous Turbine Hall, which once housed the electrical generators, is five stories high and boasts a floor area of over 55,000 square feet.

ABOVE: Tony Hawk, also known as "The Birdman," America's leading skateboarder, launched his 13-date world tour in London. Hawk, who won his first contest at the age of 11, was the world's first million-dollar-a-year professional skateboarder. He was the first person ever to achieve a "900," when the boarder spins 900 degrees in the air—equivalent to two-and-a-half turns. Hawk has frequently appeared skateboarding in movies and has launched his own computer and video game series.

OPPOSITE: Jamie Bell, chosen from 2,000 candidates for the role, appears in a scene from the movie *Billy Elliot*. The British drama based in County Durham told the story of a young aspiring dancer brought up by his father in the midst of the 1980s miners' strikes. The film, directed by Stephen Daldry, was nominated for three Academy Awards and won three BAFTA awards. In 2005 *Billy Elliot The Musical*, also directed by Daldry and featuring music composed by Elton John, opened in London. The show won 10 Tonys after opening on Broadway in 2008.

ABOVE: Sierra Leone emerges through the heat haze as an RAF Chinook fires flares to divert missile attacks. In May 2000 Operation Palliser was launched to control rebel activity from the Revolutionary United Front, to establish order and allow the peace process to continue after nine years of Civil War.

OPPOSITE: On July 25, 2000 Concorde, an icon of aviation history, crashed near Paris just after leaving Charles de Gaulle airport. All 109 people on board and four further people on the ground were killed. Investigations revealed that a titanium strip from another aircraft punctured the tire. A piece of rubber then ruptured the fuel tank and broke an electric cable causing a fire.

Daily Mail WIN £25,000 A YEAR FOR LIFE

An amateur plane-spotter captures on film the
terrible moment when a supersonic dream
became a fireball that was to kill 113 people

FLAMES OF
DISASTER

POLICE

POLICE

ABOVE: The British pop band Steps was described by songwriter Pete Waterman as like "Abba on speed" and they enjoyed phenomenal popularity with 14 successive Top 5 singles, a run that began with "One For Sorrow" in 1998. The group's name reflected their distinctive live act, where the choreography was made an integral part of the song. In 1999 they toured the US as the support act for Britney Spear's Baby One More Time tour. In 2000 they received the Brit Award for Best Selling Live Act of the year.

OPPOSITE: George Clooney promotes his latest movie *The Perfect Storm*. The American actor, producer, and director came to fame for his part in the drama *ER*, before breaking into Hollywood in *From Dusk Till Dawn*. His most famous role came in *Ocean's Eleven*, a blockbuster that was followed by two sequels. In 2006 Clooney was nominated for Best Director and Best Original Screenplay in *Good Night, and Good Luck* and Best Supporting Actor in *Syriana*. Two years later he received a further nomination for Best Actor in *Michael Clayton*.

2000

RIGHT: English singer and songwriter David Gray on stage. Gray rose to fame after the release of the album *White Ladder* in 1999, which spent more than 150 weeks on the UK album charts, reaching the number-one slot more than two years after its release. In the US, the album spent a year on the *Billboard* 200 chart.

OPPOSITE: Coldplay record in a TV studio. The band formed in London in 1998 and shot to fame with their first single, "Yellow." Their debut album *Parachutes*, released in 2000, was nominated for the Mercury Prize in the UK, and was eventually awarded the Grammy for the Best Alternative Music Album in 2002. *Parachutes* was soon followed by Grammy-winning *A Rush of Blood to the Head*, one of the best-selling albums of the decade. The band are active supporters of charity organizations, including Amnesty International and Oxfam's Make Trade Fair campaign.

ABOVE: Eighty-year-old Jim Ellis-Beech, an army physical training instructor for 24 years, captured during a bungee jump. He had hoped to gain a place in the *Guinness Book of Records* for being the oldest person to complete six hazardous activities in a day; wingwalking, bungee jumping, looping the loop, completing an army assault course, abseiling down a cliff, and parachute jumping. Unfortunately the feat was not recognized as a record.

OPPOSITE: Photographers train their lenses on the balcony of Buckingham Palace to catch a glimpse of the Queen Mother on her 100th birthday. Forty thousand well-wishers gathered in The Mall as the Royal Family made their traditional appearance on the balcony after a birthday lunch. Among the many events to celebrate the occasion, the Queen Mother received the customary telegram from her daughter and the Royal Bank of Scotland issued a commemorative £20 banknote.

2000

RIGHT: USA's Michael Johnson qualifies from his heat in the men's 400 meters with Great Britain's Sean Baldock in the next lane at the Sydney Olympics. Johnson went on to take the gold in the 400 meters and also in the 4 x 400 meters relay. In June 2008, Johnson voluntarily returned the relay gold medal after Antonio Pettigrew, Johnson's team-mate who ran the second leg, admitted that he took performance-enhancing drugs between 1997 and 2001.

OPPOSITE: The city of Sydney in Australia is ready for the start of the 2000 Olympic Games. With the motto Share the Spirit, 199 nations took part with 10,651 athletes competing in 28 different sports. Governor-General Sir William Deane opened the games and in a spectacular conclusion to the opening ceremony, the final torchbearer, Australian sprinter Cathy Freeman, walked across a circular pool of water and ignited the cauldron through the water, surrounding herself with fire.

OPPOSITE: (L–R) British rowers James Cracknell, Steve Redgrave, Tim Foster, and Matthew Pinsent pictured after winning the coxless four gold medal. After this achievement Steve Redgrave became one of the few athletes to win gold medals at five consecutive Olympic Games. He also had three Commonwealth Games golds and nine World Championship golds in his collection.

ABOVE: America's Marion Jones celebrates as she wins the gold medal in the women's 100 meters final in a time of 10.75 seconds. Jones also won gold in the 200 meters and 4 x 400 meters relay and bronze in the long jump and 4 x 100 meters relay. However, she later admitted to taking performance-enhancing drugs, was given a two-year ban and stripped of her Olympic medals.

2000

RIGHT: Britain's Denise Lewis flies through the air in the long jump section of the women's heptathlon. Achieving 6584 points overall, Lewis won the gold medal over the Russian Yelena Prokhorova, who was awarded silver, and bronze medalist Natallia Sazanovich from Belarus.

OPPOSITE: Photographers wait for the start of the men's 100 meters final. The eventual gold medallist was Maurice Green from the United States, who won in a time of 9.87 seconds. Ato Boldon from Trinidad and Tobago took silver while Obadele Thompson from Barbados won the bronze.

Sydney 2000

ABOVE: Little-known American Rulon Gardner (right) beat Alexandre Karline, the Russian favorite in the 130-kilogram Greco-Roman wrestling event, winning the gold medal. Dmitry Debelka from Belarus was third. Russian athletes dominated most of the wrestling events winning six gold medals.

OPPOSITE: Konstantinos Kenteris won Greece's only gold medal of the Olympics in the men's 200 meters, with Britain's Darren Campbell finishing in second place. The Greek was forced to withdraw from the 2004 games in Athens because of doping offenses.

Available Now

£2.00

BIG BROTHER

RIGHT: Flowers lie on the track at the scene of the Hatfield rail crash that occurred in October 2000. A train traveling from London toward Leeds with more than 100 passengers lost two coaches when it derailed north of the capital. Four people were killed and another 70 injured.

OPPOSITE: Originating in the Netherlands, the *Big Brother* format was picked up by broadcasters across the globe. Here members of the UK Channel 4's first series are pictured at their book-signing. Forty thousand people applied to be in the original show which ran for nine weeks and was an instant success. An average of 4.5 million viewers tuned in each week with this figure rising to 10 million for the final. The eventual winner was Craig Phillips (second from right) who won £70,000 but donated his winnings to a friend with Down's syndrome who needed a heart and lung transplant. In the US, wheelchair basketball player Eddie McGee won the first series.

2000

OPPOSITE: The remains of the Ostruznica Bridge which spanned the River Danube between parts of Belgrade city, bombed by NATO at the end of the Kosovo War. The Serbian dictator Slobodan Milosevic was forced to end military operations and after the 2000 presidential elections power was handed over to Vojislav Kostunica. Milosevic was charged with war crimes but during the trial was found dead in his cell from a heart attack.

RIGHT: Scandal, the luxury perfume store in the center of Belgrade, was destroyed by demonstrators because it was owned by former President Milosevic's wife.

2000

OPPOSITE: Scenes in Ramalla on the day of the Egyptian peace talks in October 2000. An emergency summit held at Sharm-el-Sheikh was attended by world leaders including US President Bill Clinton, Hosni Mubarak, the Egyptian president, Ehud Barak, the Israeli Prime Minister, and Yasser Arafat, the Palestinian leader.

LEFT: Children pictured at the funeral of a fellow Palestinian on the day of the Egyptian peace talks.

ABOVE: Frank Lampard pictured in the boot room during a training session at West Ham Football Club. Lampard had joined the club where his father was assistant coach and remained there until 2001 when he moved to Chelsea for a fee of £11 million.

OPPOSITE: Miss World contestants were filmed in the Maldives prior to the final at the Millennium Dome in London at the end of November 2000. Ninety-five girls took part in the 50th Miss World pageant and judges included Stephanie Beacham, Lulu, and Errol Brown. The winner was Priyanka Chopra from India with Giorgia Palmas from Italy, second.

46

2000

RIGHT: Prince Charles stands outside the Rovers Return pub on the set of the television soap opera *Coronation Street*. During his visit he watched the final rehearsals for an hour-long live episode due to be screened that evening to mark the program's 40th anniversary.

OPPOSITE: Bill Clinton, pictured during the last few weeks of his presidency with ally Tony Blair. At home, Clinton's vice president Al Gore was in the final stage of losing the presidential race to George W. Bush. In the last hours of the election on November 7, irregularities in counting the votes in the state of Florida delayed a clear result until a Supreme Court ruling on December 12 declared in Bush's favor. The margin in Florida was barely 500 votes and overall Gore polled more votes across all the states than his opponent. The international community looked on in some amazement as one US President who narrowly avoided impeachment handed over government to the next, who apparently achieved office without actually winning the election.

2001

ABOVE: Renée Zellweger in *Bridget Jones's Diary*, the hit movie about an eventful year in the life of a single, Chardonnay-swigging, chain-smoking, lovelorn, thirty-something woman, which also starred Hugh Grant as her philandering boss and Colin Firth as an aloof lawyer she comes to love.

OPPOSITE: A scene from the first film in the *Lord of the Rings* trilogy, *The Fellowship of the Ring*, which was released on December 19. The movie was highly acclaimed and considered to be very faithful to J.R.R. Tolkien's original book. It went on to earn $870 million, making it the second-highest grossing film of 2001.

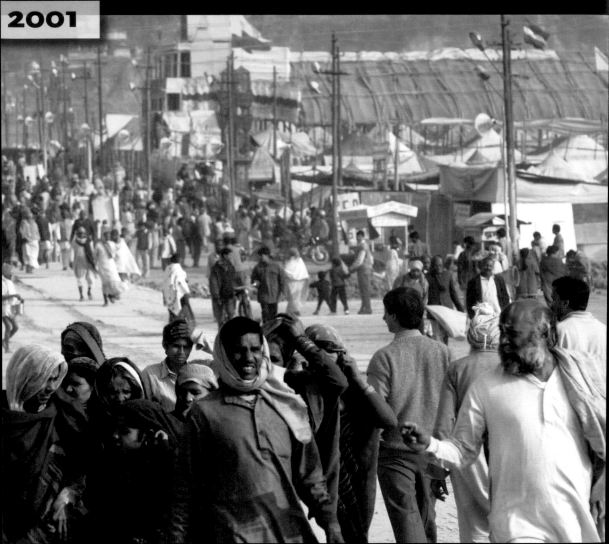

2001

ABOVE: A bandleader heading a procession arriving at the sacred Hindu festival Maha Kumbh Mela in January. The Kumbh Mela pilgrimage occurs four times every twelve years—once at each of four locations—but every twelve years the Maha (great) Kumbh Mela is held at Allahabad at the sacred confluence of three holy rivers: the Ganges, Yamuna and Saraswati.

OPPOSITE: Pilgrims at Maha Kumbh Mela in Allahabad in 2001, at which it is estimated 60 million people came to bathe in the Ganges—making it the largest pilgrimage gathering around the world.

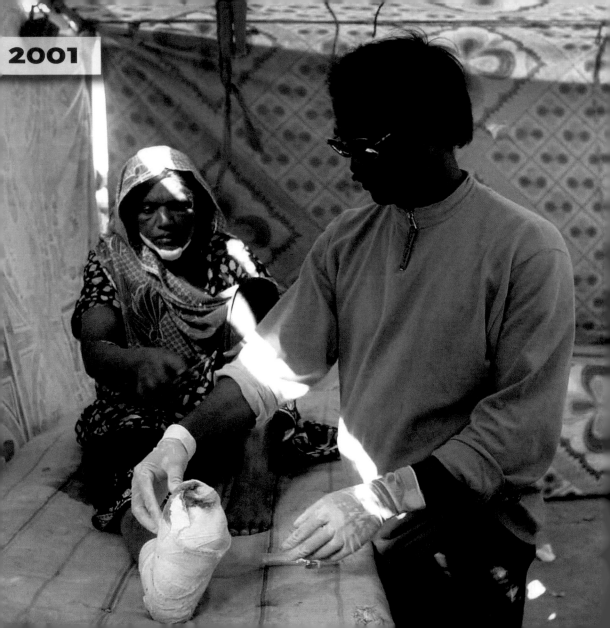
2001

OPPOSITE: Dr Jeevan Bhurti attends the wounded at a temporary hospital in Buju, India. The town had been the epicenter of a massive earthquake on January 26, India's Republic Day, which killed more than 25,000 people and destroyed nearly 400,000 homes throughout the Indian state of Gujarat and areas of eastern Pakistan.

RIGHT: Five days after the earthquake bodies still hidden under rubble had started to decompose, and workers had to wear masks because of the smell. Food and water supplies had been destroyed, which made a return to normal life even more difficult.

2001

LEFT: The aftermath of the Selby rail crash on February 28, in which two trains collided after a Land-Rover towing a trailer veered off the M62 motorway in North Yorkshire, down an embankment and onto the railroad track below. Ten people were killed and 82 injured, and the driver of the car—who was suspected of having fallen asleep at the wheel—was later jailed for five years.

OPPOSITE: In February, foot-and-mouth broke out in UK livestock for the first time in 20 years; during the course of the epidemic there were 2,030 confirmed cases in the UK and Northern Ireland but around six million animals were slaughtered. Television screens around the world were full of footage of burning carcasses, causing havoc to Britain's tourist industry.

2001

RIGHT: Sir Elton John (right) and partner David Furnish arrive at Christie's auction rooms for the preview of 20 classic cars from the star's collection due to go under the hammer the following week, which eventually realized nearly £2 million. The star was obviously not feeling the pinch—although the previous year there were reports that he spent almost £40 million over a 20-month period, including £293,000 on flowers, he had just made the "rich lists" with estimated earnings of £26 million a year.

OPPOSITE: On March 19 Michael Jackson was inducted into the Rock and Roll Hall of Fame. The following July he released "Rock My World," the first single from his forthcoming album *Invincible*, which turned out to be the last to be released during his lifetime. Just before the album came out he played a 30th Anniversary concert at Madison Square Garden in New York to celebrate his 30 years as a solo artist—at which he appeared on stage with his brothers for the first time since 1984.

ABOVE: *Moulin Rouge* was the opening night movie at the 2001 Cannes Film Festival held in the South of France in May. The musical starred Nicole Kidman and Ewan McGregor, seen here in a publicity photograph, and was a smash success making over US$57 million in the US and $120 million worldwide.

OPPOSITE: In 2001 Leigh Zimmerman, one of the Broadway cast members, joined the London cast of *Chicago* as Velma Kelly. The West End version of the famous musical ran for nine years in the Adelphi Theatre then transferred to the Cambridge Theatre. In New York the show has run continuously since 1996, although it was first a hit in the mid 1970s.

CHICAGO
THE MUSICAL

2001

RIGHT: Lord and Lady Archer arrive at the Old Bailey in July, where the novelist and British politician was later found guilty of perjury and perverting justice. In 1987 the *Daily Star* had printed a story revealing that he had an affair with a prostitute, paid her hush money, and falsified records. Outraged at the alleged slander to his good name, Archer had sued and won, but the paper's story was now proved to be accurate. He was sentenced to four years in jail.

OPPOSITE: Bill Clinton's second term in office ended on January 20, 2001 but he continued campaigning for the goals he had set out while in office. Moving to New York, he helped his wife Hillary become elected to the Senate in 2001, launching her official political career, which would culminate as a presidential candidate in the 2008 election race against fellow-democrat Barack Obama.

2001

LEFT: David Duval kisses the claret jug trophy after his victory in the 2001 Open Championship at the Royal Lytham & St Anne's Golf Club, England. His first major win, it made him the sixth American in the last seven years to triumph at golf's oldest championship.

OPPOSITE: Goran Ivanisevic holds aloft the trophy after winning the Men's Final at the Wimbledon Championships on July 9. He beat Australia's Patrick Rafter 6-3 3-6 6-3 2-6 9-7 after a thrilling final game; it was Ivanisevic's fourth Wimbledon final and he was the first wild card to make it through to the final.

2001

RIGHT: US President George W. Bush visits the Cabinet War Rooms in London during a brief stopover in the UK prior to traveling to the G8 conference in Genoa.

OPPOSITE: Protestors at the G8 summit in Genoa, Italy, in July marching toward the exclusion zone; the center of town had been declared off-limits for non-residents and surrounded by a barricade. The protest included an estimated 200,000 demonstrators and over 400 were injured in clashes with police. On one of the final days, 23-year-old activist Carlo Giuliani was shot dead by a carabinieri officer, who was later judged to have been acting in self-defense.

2001

The Mail ON SUNDAY

30-PAGE SPECIAL REPORT

Bush prepares America for 'long conflict'

'WE ARE AT WAR'

- Broad and sustained campaign to eradicate the evil of terrorism
- Series of decisive actions against those who harbour terrorists
- America's enemies have chosen their own destruction

Smoke pours from the south tower of the World Trade Center in New York as it burns after terrorists had crashed a hijacked jet into it on September 11. A second jet had already hit the north tower. More than 2,750 people died in the attack, including both those on the two planes and on the ground. A third jet hit the Pentagon, with the loss of 184 lives. In a fourth jet, which was making for Washington, passengers attempted to overpower the hijackers and the plane crashed into a field with the loss of 40 lives. Within hours both towers had collapsed and the subsequent fires caused structural failure, destroying the Marriott Hotel also in the complex and causing a thick cloud of dust and debris to roll along surrounding streets.

ABOVE: The front page of the *Mail on Sunday* on September 16, with a photograph of President George W. Bush.

2001

Daily Mail
30 PAGES OF PICTURES AND REPORTS

TEARS FOR AMERICA

ABOVE: Flowers being laid at the statue of Theodore Roosevelt in Grosvenor Square in London, in memory of those who died in New York.

RIGHT: The front page of the *Daily Mail* on September 15, with a photograph of Her Majesty Queen Elizabeth II crying at the memorial service for the victims of the terrorist attacks in America.

A New Yorker checks out the hundreds of posters displayed at the Belle Vue Hospital in the city, which were put up by families hoping for news of their missing loved ones after the twin towers terrorist attack. Weeks after the attack, only around 1,600 victims had been recovered from the debris and positively identified.

2001

ABOVE: On September 11, 7 World Trade Center also collapsed, having been damaged by falling debris from the twin towers and subsequent fires. The three remaining buildings in the complex were so badly damaged that they had to be demolished. The site was cleared over the following eight months, with shifts working 24 hours a day. Within hours of the attack, the FBI had established that responsibility lay with Osama bin Laden and the Islamic terrorist organization al-Qaeda.

OPPOSITE: An anti-American protest by Islamic Fundamentalist supporters in the Khyber Bazaar in Peshawar, Pakistan. However, the Pakistan government backed the US in their war against terrorism, arresting hundreds of alleged al-Qaeda members and handing them over for interrogation.

2001

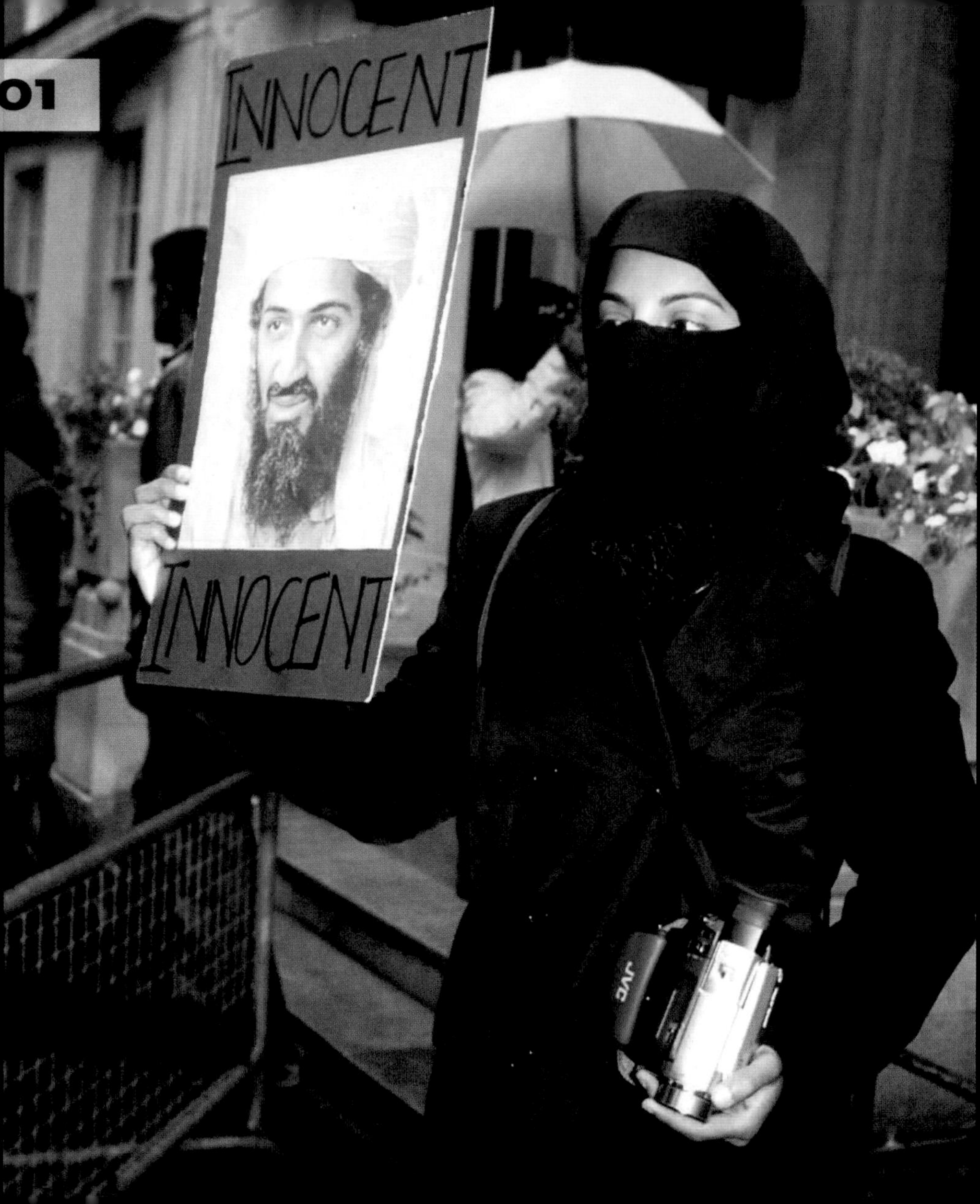

ABOVE: Delegates and their advisors at Bagram Airport on their way to a conference in Bonn, Germany, to discuss the future of Afghanistan. The United Nations-backed conference included the four main Afghan groups—but not the Taliban—as well as representatives from a number of interested countries, including the US, India, Pakistan, and Iran. The peace process that began there became known as the Petersberg Process, but it was not successfully completed until February 2006.

OPPOSITE: A woman protests in support of Osama bin Laden, who initially denied any involvement in the 9/11 attack on New York. Some believe that he really did not instigate it, and only later decided to claim responsibility to increase the perceived importance of al-Qaeda.

ABOVE: Afghan refugee children as young as three laboring in a brickworks in Peshawar, Pakistan. In September 2001, the UN held a Special Session on Children to discuss progress in the last decade since the World Summit for Children, with a priority being the problem of child labor. UNICEF had estimated that there were still at least 250 million children between the ages of five and fourteen working for a living in developing countries, at least half of them full time.

OPPOSITE: Anti-American demonstrators in Peshawar, Pakistan, near the Afghan border. On October 7, the US had launched an attack on Afghanistan, which was ruled by the militant Islamic Taliban, launching bombs and cruise missiles near several key Afghan cities, including Kabul and Kandahar. Al-Qaeda had military bases and training camps dotted throughout Afghanistan's forbidding central and northern mountain ranges.

2001

LEFT: An armed guard keeps watch high in the Afghan mountains. President Bush had ordered the air strikes after Taliban leaders refused US demands to close terrorist training camps, hand over al-Qaeda leaders, and return all foreign nationals who were being detained. However, the raids also had a humanitarian aspect as planes dropped food, medicine, and supplies to the starving and suffering people of Afghanistan.

OPPOSITE: Taliban soldiers defecting across the River Pyanji in Northern Afghanistan. After the city of Mazari Sharif in northern Afghanistan fell to US/Northern Alliance forces on November 9, many local groups switched loyalties from the Taliban to the Northern Alliance, which was a coalition of various Afghan factions that had united to fight against the Taliban.

2001

ABOVE: A group of Muslims demonstrate their support for Islam. Some extremist groups reported that scores of young British Muslims were signing up to join the Taliban fighters in Afghanistan, even though some recent volunteers had already been killed in US bombing raids.

OPPOSITE: Pro-Taliban demonstrators hang an effigy of President Bush in Peshawar, Pakistan. Religious leaders in the North-West Frontier Province of Pakistan had sent students to fight alongside the Taliban in the battle to take control of Afghanistan in the late 1990s, and later the Taliban hardline ideology had taken hold in some areas.

OPPOSITE: Hundreds of people come down from the hills around Bethlehem to attend the funeral of Palestinian martyr Atef Abayat. In October, violence had intensified across the West Bank after Israeli Tourism Minister Rehavam Ze'evi was assassinated in East Jerusalem in retaliation for the assassination of PFLP leader Abu Ali Mustafa in August. Israeli tanks and troops moved into Palestinian territory, and trouble flared in Bethlehem when Abayat, a local leader of the Tanzim militia, and two colleagues were killed in a car bomb attack that was blamed on Israel.

ABOVE: Later in October, two Palestinian gunmen opened fire from a car at random, killing four women and wounding many others in the coastal city of Hadera, north of Tel Aviv, hours after an Israeli soldier was shot dead in the same area. One of the gunmen lies in the road after being shot dead by Israeli police.

2001

RIGHT: The front page of the London *Evening Standard* on November 12, showing houses on fire in the residential district of Queens, New York City, after an American Airlines airbus crashed just after takeoff from JFK airport. The crash killed all 260 people on board and five people on the ground, and was apparently caused by the tail fin, the rudder that was attached to it, and both engines falling off the airplane shortly after it was airborne.

OPPOSITE: In June 2001 Tony Blair led his party to a convincing election victory and a second term in government, with a very large parliamentary majority.

WEST END FINAL

Evening Standard

LONDON, MONDAY, 12 NOVEMBER 2001   www.thisislondon.co.uk   Incorporating THE EVENING NEWS   35p

'Hundreds dead' as plane hits homes

NEW YORK JET CRASH

Sky TV shows firemen at the scene as flames tear through houses set alight by the fireball which erupted when the American Airlines Airbus plunged on to the Queens district of New York

● HUNDREDS of people died today when an American Airlines Airbus crashed on take-off from JFK onto a residential area of New York.

● There were immediate fears of terrorism. The FBI reported an explosion aboard the plane. But an accident has not been ruled out.

● All 255 people aboard the plane are feared to have died as are more people in the buildings in Queens engulfed in flames after it hit.

● New York's airports were immediately closed and the city put on full security alert.
Full Story: Pages 2 & 3. Pictures: Back Page

STANDARD REPORTER SEES ALLIANCE BREAK TALIBAN LINES AT KABUL: PAGES 4 & 5

Children play cricket in the street in New Delhi, India. In December, the England cricket team arrived in India for a series of three Test matches, which India won 1–0 after two matches were drawn. The English side was inexperienced and a freak rainstorm had washed out the last two days, so England's team captain, Nasser Hussain, was buoyant as they left for the UK, telling reporters they had played well and only been narrowly defeated.

Local guards watch the 1st Test match in the India v England series, on December 3 in Mohali, India. The score in the 1st innings was England 238 all out, India 469 all out. In the second innings it was England 235 all out, India 5–0, and India won the match by 10 wickets. The Indian team included Sachin Tendulkar, who most cricket experts agreed was the best batsman in the world.

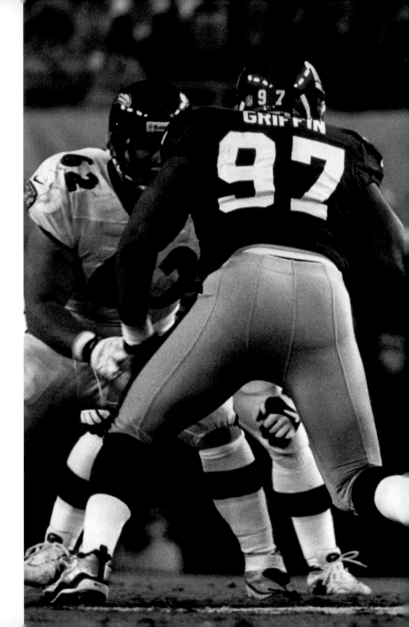

2001

Baltimore Ravens quarterback Trent Dilfer fades to pass in Super Bowl XXXV. The Ravens defeated the New York Giants 34–7 in Tampa, Florida. The Ravens became the third wild card team to win the Super Bowl— the second in four years. And the city of Baltimore had its first Super Bowl title in 30 years.

2001

ABOVE: The Afghan version of polo, with two teams of 12 riders and using the stuffed carcass of a small calf, being played outside the National Stadium in Kabul. During the reign of the Taliban this was where public executions had taken place, but after the October invasion by the US their rule had been broken and by the end of December many had dispersed.

OPPOSITE: Country Fire Authority firefighter Brent Gazzanign hoses flames during a back-burning operation near houses in Heathcote, south of Sydney, Australia, on December 27. Thousands of firefighters had been fighting fierce bush fires that had been ringing the city for three days, but they continued to burn for nearly three weeks. Approximately 740,000 acres were burnt, 121 homes destroyed and 36 more badly damaged. The first blaze was thought to have been started by an imperfectly extinguished campfire, but arsonists started some later ones.

OPPOSITE: Young Beatles fan Ruth Bishop signs the book of condolences inside the Cavern Club in Liverpool, after the death of former band member George Harrison on November 29 in Hollywood Hills, California. He had developed throat cancer in 1997, and despite extensive treatment it spread to his lungs.

RIGHT: Sir Paul McCartney, seen with his then-girlfriend Heather Mills, said: "I am devastated and very, very sad. We knew he'd been ill for a long time. He was a lovely guy and a very brave man and had a wonderful sense of humor. He is really just my baby brother. I loved him very much and I will miss him greatly."

ABOVE: One of the most unlikely contests in the history of sport was held at Wimbledon Stadium on May 22; the world's first race between a grayhound and a pigeon. The unique battle of the species took place over the final 80 meters of the Derby course under normal racing conditions. In the blue jacket, running for grayhound racing, was the 1999 Derby quarter-finalist and brilliant sprinter Athea Storm, a top-class open racer with a career record of 12 wins from 20 starts. In the red jacket, flying for the pigeon fanciers, was UK Show Sprint titleholder Speckled Jim, a champion racing pigeon, who was undefeated in 27 races over sprint trips. The race was won by Athea Storm.

OPPOSITE: US President George W. Bush (left) with Her Majesty Queen Elizabeth II, US First Lady Laura Bush, and the Duke of Edinburgh. The President and his wife had been invited to lunch at Buckingham Palace on their first visit to the UK, where they had stopped off while traveling to the G8 summit in Genoa, Italy.

2001

LEFT: Children at Jalozai Refugee Camp in Pakistan. Shela (center), a 12-year-old Afghan refugee, sold balloons on the street to support her family. Many Afghans had fled their country when the Taliban took over, but after they were removed from power at the end of 2001 many began to return.

OPPOSITE: Britain's Prime Minister Tony Blair shakes hands with Palestinian President Yasser Arafat on the steps of 10 Downing Street in London on October 15. The two leaders met to discuss the stalled Middle East peacemaking process and the recent US-led strikes on Afghanistan.

Taliban prisoners being held by US Special Forces ready for interrogation. Thousands of Taliban fighters had surrendered to General Dostum's forces, part of the Northern Alliance, and were transported to a prison near the town of Shibarghan. Later some reported that they were locked in closed metal shipping containers for days and given no food or water.

Two women in burqas study a selection of lipsticks. Afghanistan had previously been fairly liberal, but during the Taliban's seven-year rule women were banned from jobs, girls forbidden to attend schools or universities, and adult females were required to wear a burqa when out in public. Men were required to have a beard, short hair, and to wear a head covering. A wide variety of hitherto everyday activities, such as listening to music or watching television, were banned.

The unfinished Serbian Orthodox Cathedral Church, Christ the Savior, in the center of Pristina, Kosovo, is guarded round the clock by British troops forming part of the UN peacekeeping force KFOR. Intended as a further demonstration by the Serbs of their supremacy over Kosovo's Albanian Muslim population, the brick and concrete structure was pitched next to the national library on ground owned by Pristina University and should have been completed in 1999. In fact, following the NATO bombing of Kosovo and the withdrawal of Serbian forces, nearly all of the Serb civilian population fled the province while Albanian exiles flooded back to their homes, creating an Albanian majority. Orthodox churches became a target for Albanian vengeance and most were vandalized or destroyed.

Potters Bar

Welcome to
Potters Bar

Canada Life™
● Retirement Income
● Protection
● Investments

On May 10, 2002 a West Anglia Great Northern train service from London's King's Cross station, bound for King's Lynn, Norfolk, derailed at high speed in Potters Bar station, a short distance from London, leaving part of the train wedged between the platform and building structures. Seven people were killed in the accident, six aboard the train and one under the bridge hit by the carriages. Over 70 others were injured, 11 of them seriously.

2002

ABOVE: Former president of Serbia and the Federal Republic of Yugoslavia, Slobodan Milosevic, wears an inscrutable expression as he appears before the UN War Crimes Tribunal in The Hague, Netherlands on Tuesday, February 12, 2002, the first day of his trial for alleged atrocities and genocide during the break-up of Yugoslavia. Milosevic denied the validity of the court but conducted his own defense over the five-year trial, dying of a heart attack before he could be sentenced. His demise appeared to have been hastened by his refusal to take prescribed medications.

OPPOSITE: New York Mayor Rudi Giuliani pictured with HRH the Duke of York on February 13, displaying the honorary knighthood he had just received from the Queen. A contingent of New Yorkers arrived in the UK to receive honors, including police commissioner Bernard Kerik and former fire commissioner Thomas van Essen. Giuliani brought with him his executive assistant, Elizabeth Petrone, whose fireman husband, Captain Terry Hatton, died on 9/11.

2002

LEFT: The funeral of Queen Elizabeth the Queen Mother took place on Tuesday 9, April 2002. The coffin of the Queen Mother is borne into Westminster Abbey on the shoulders of members of the Queen's Guard. Born Elizabeth Bowes-Lyon, the Queen Mother was one of the most popular members of the royal family and there was great mourning when she passed away on March 30, aged 101.

OPPOSITE: More than 200,000 people waited in line to pay their last respects to the Queen Mother who lay in state in Westminster Hall. Prior to the funeral service, the Abbey's tenor bell tolled 101 times, once for each year of her life. After the ceremony, more than a million people lined the funeral cortège's route from Westminster to Windsor Castle where, during a private family service in St George's Chapel, her body was interred alongside her late husband King George VI. In accordance with her wishes, her funeral wreath was placed on the tomb of the Unknown Soldier, mirroring a gesture made on her wedding day decades earlier.

2002

RIGHT: Bryan McFadden found success as one fifth of Irish pop band, Westlife. In 2002 the band released their 11th UK number one single, "Unbreakable" which was followed by the number one album of the same name. That year McFadden married Atomic Kitten star Kerry Katona, with whom he had two daughters. In spring 2004 McFadden left the band, just before they were due to embark on their fourth world tour, to spend more time with his family and concentrate on his solo projects. His first solo single, "Real to Me" debuted at number one. The time spent with his family led to separation from Katona by the end of 2004 and divorce in 2006.

OPPOSITE: Pierce Brosnan puckers up with his *Die Another Day* co-stars, Rosamund Pike (left) and Halle Berry. The twentieth Bond film and Brosnan's last as 007, its release marked the 40th anniversary of the spy franchise begun in 1962 by Sean Connery in *Dr. No*. The screenplay was not based on an Ian Fleming story but was novelized by writer Raymond Benson. The movie became the highest grossing James Bond film until *Casino Royale* knocked it off its top spot in 2006.

2002

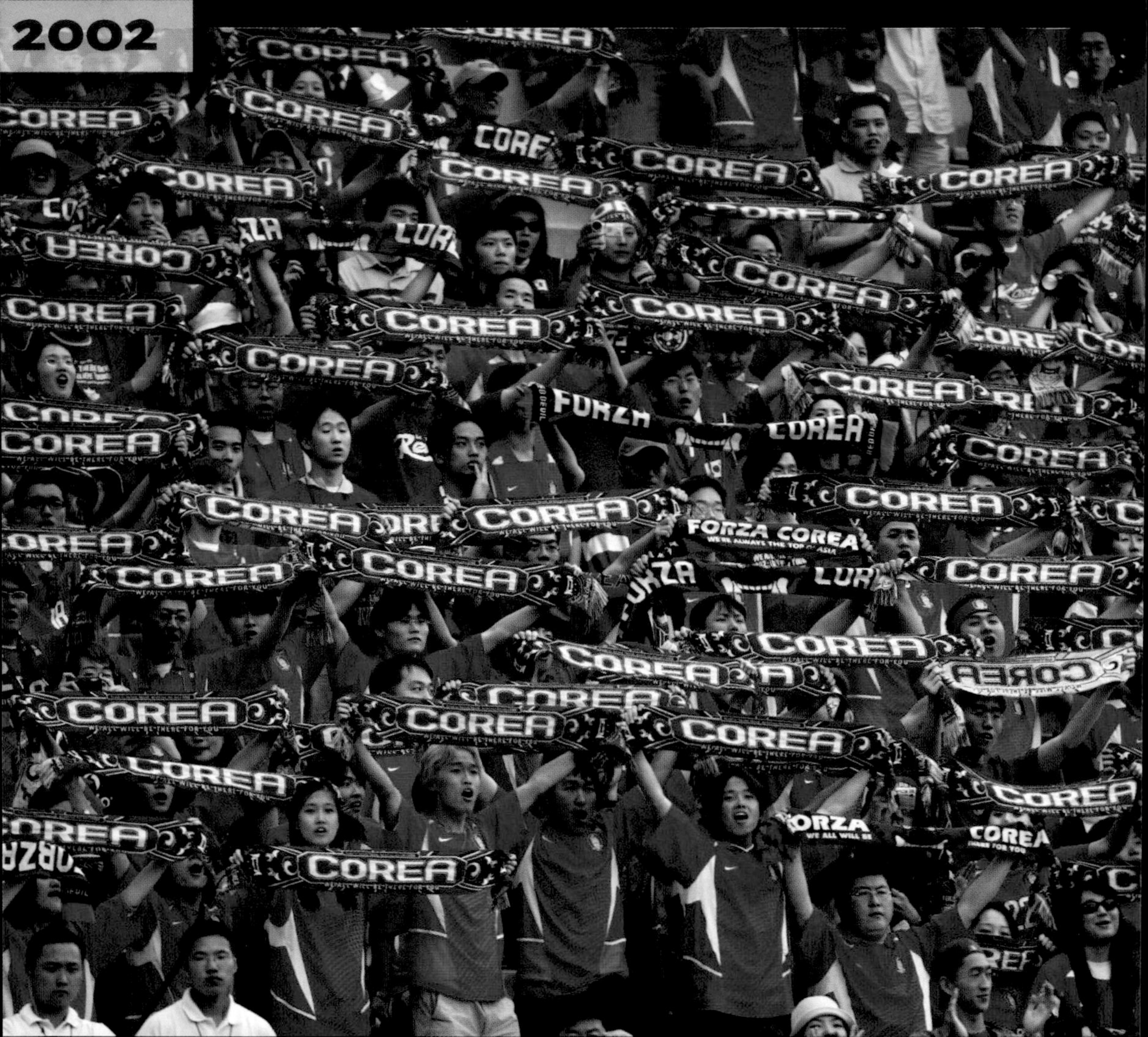

ABOVE: US special forces spearheaded the move to eradicate al-Quaeda from Afghanistan, where they had been harbored by the Taliban; the attack on various cities and training camps began on October 7, 2001 and by November 12, the Taliban forces had fled the capital Kabul to escape the advancing Northern Alliance supported by US and British forces. It would be many years before a semblance of normality could return to Kabul. Here Kabul Zoo's Afghan bear Donatella, who had her nose destroyed by a Taliban soldier with a bayonet, plays with her keeper Shir Agha Omar after returning to her newly repaired enclosure.

OPPOSITE: The FIFA World Cup 2002 was jointly hosted by South Korea and Japan, the first time the tournament had been held in Asia or by joint nations. The competition kicked off on May 31 to a surprise start in Seoul World Cup Stadium with Senegal beating the defending champions France with a 1-0 score. Here South Korean fans cheer on their home side at Daegu World Cup Stadium, where the team drew in their match with the US.

ABOVE: On the final day of the Queen's Golden Jubilee weekend, June 4, around 1,000,000 people lined London's Mall and assembled outside Buckingham Palace to enjoy the celebrations which included a parade that concluded with 5,000 people from all over the Commonwealth passing in front of the Queen, dressed in their national costumes. From the palace balcony the Queen and the rest of the Royal Family watched a dramatic fly-past by the Royal Air Force that included every aircraft in service and Concorde flanked by the RAF's formation flying team The Red Arrows.

OPPOSITE: Blues guitarist Eric Clapton performs during the Party at the Palace concert, which formed part of Queen Elizabeth's Golden Jubilee celebrations at Buckingham Palace from June 1 to 4. The evening concert on Monday, June 3 showcased 50 years of contemporary music and commenced with a dramatic guitar solo performance of "God Save the Queen" by Queen's Brian May playing on the roof of the palace. Around 12,000 members of the public, selected by lottery, attended the concert, which featured music from Sir Paul McCartney, Annie Lennox, Tom Jones, Tony Bennett, Cliff Richard, and Brian Wilson among many others.

2002

luvlee
Jublee

RIGHT: The 17th Commonwealth Games were held in Manchester, England, during July and August 2002, bringing together athletes from 72 member states of the Commonwealth of Nations. It was the biggest sporting event ever held in the United Kingdom and provided a focus for the re-generation of Manchester in the wake of the IRA bombing in 1996. The Manchester Aquatic Centre was purpose-built for the event; this remarkable picture of the women's 10-meter-high board won Andy Hooper the "best shot of the Games" award.

OPPOSITE: Crowds packed into The Mall, celebrating the Queen's 50 years on the throne in a national display unmatched since the death of Diana, Princess of Wales five years before. Across the country the exuberance of the weekend brought out the British spirit of pageantry and the longstanding tradition of street partying.

2002

ABOVE: In the World Cup Tournament final held in the International Stadium, Yokohama, Japan on June 30, Brazil met Germany, beating them 2-0, giving Brazil their fifth World Cup win. The popularity of the team brought a wide range of supporters to the game as well as across the world via video broadcast. These young Brazilians put on a lively samba to encourage their national team.

OPPOSITE: In a second-round match of the 2002 FIFA World Cup tournament played in Kobe, Japan, between Brazil and Belgium, Brazil midfielder Rivaldo waves his shirt in delight as he leads team celebrations after scoring the opening goal. The final score was Brazil 2 Belgium 0.

2002

RIGHT: Australia's Lleyton Hewitt holds up the winner's trophy after his victory over Argentina's David Nalbandian in the men's singles final at the Wimbledon tennis championships on July 7, 2002. Hewitt won in straight sets, 6-1, 6-3, 6-2. A highly competitive player on all surfaces, Hewitt's career peaked in 2001 when he was ranked World Number 1 but his solid performance in 2002, winning several other major titles, kept him in top-rank position for the second year in succession.

OPPOSITE: In July 2002 Venus Williams won the first Grand Slam singles title of her career at the Wimbledon tennis championships, defeating Lindsay Davenport in the final.

2002

ABOVE: Her Majesty Queen Elizabeth II and the Duke of Edinburgh wave to crowds from the balcony at Buckingham Palace after the annual Trooping the Color to mark the Queen's official birthday.

OPPOSITE: President George W. Bush (second left) and his wife Laura leave St. Ann's Episcopal Church, Kennebunkport, Maine, with his mother Barbara and father, George H.W. Bush (second right), the former President. Bush took office in 2001 and after the September 11 bombing responded by announcing a War on Terrorism, launching an attack on Afghanistan and another against Iraq in 2003.

2002

LEFT: Sophie Ellis-Bextor's extraordinary china-doll looks set her apart visually; musically her eclectic style included pop, dance, and electronic influences. Her first album, *Read My Lips,* released in 2001, made it to number two and resulted in four top 20 hits, including the massive European hit "Murder on the Dancefloor"—a top selling single of 2002.

OPPOSITE: Shakira, the Colombian-born latin singing star, emerged on the international scene with her 2001 breakthrough album *Laundry Service,* which took her from a mainly Hispanic audience to world stardom. Her larger-than-life stage performance includes an exuberant dance style, which benefited from her part-Lebanese background that encouraged her to learn belly-dancing to overcome shyness. Shakira is a talented business-woman who also finds time to support humanitarian causes, frequently performing for charity events, as in this photograph; she also represents UNICEF as a global Goodwill Ambassador.

ABOVE: In 2002 it was announced that Simon Cowell, already a judge on the British reality TV show, *Pop Idol*, was to also judge the US version of the show, *American Idol*. Cowell had quickly became known for his blunt and scathing comments in the first UK series when he joined Pete Waterman, Nicki Chapman, and Neil "Dr" Fox on the judging panel. The winner of the British show was Will Young, whose debut single went on to sell 1.7 million copies.

OPPOSITE: Tobey Maguire as Peter Parker in the first of the series of *Spiderman* films. Released in 2002, it co-starred Kirsten Dunst and was proclaimed the third-highest-grossing movie of the year. Maguire followed this success with the highly-acclaimed film *Seabiscuit*, in which he played the role of jockey John M. "Red" Pollard. The movie was nominated for seven Academy Awards including Best Picture..

2002

ABOVE: Matt Damon in the spy film *The Bourne Identity*, based on the novel by Robert Ludlum. Damon played amnesiac Jason Bourne in the first film of the eventual trilogy. Damon's career had been launched when he co-wrote and starred in *Good Will Hunting*, which scooped him an Academy Award for Best Original Screenplay. This was followed by further success with *Saving Private Ryan*, *The Talented Mr. Ripley*, and the *Ocean's* series.

OPPOSITE: Tommy Lee Jones (right) and Will Smith in *Men in Black II*, the second science-fiction comedy based on the comic book by Lowell Cunningham. Both men were following on from major film successes the previous year. Smith had starred in *Ali*, a portrayal of the boxer Muhammad Ali, which won Smith an Academy Award for Best Actor, while Jones played Clay Shaw in *JFK*, receiving a nomination for Best Actor in a Supporting Role.

ABOVE: By May 2002, Ground Zero, the site of the former twin towers of the World Trade Center in New York City had finally been cleared, but it was to be another three years before the Medical Examiner's office ended its task of identifying any human remains that had been buried in the debris. Soon after the attack President Bush announced his intention to redevelop the site and Governor Pataki established a new corporation to oversee the rebuilding process.

OPPOSITE: The euro coins and notes had come into circulation on January 1, 2002 and were adopted by 12 European countries, including France and Germany, but the United Kingdom had chosen to negotiate an exemption. Here euro supporters Kevin Whately and Eddie Izzard join demonstrators at the Gap store in Oxford Street to show how much less you would receive when paying in pounds; the store displayed prices in both currencies but would only accept sterling.

ABOVE: United Nations Chief Weapons Inspector Hans Blix talks to the media in Vienna after a first round of talks with Iraqi officials to discuss the resumption of the search for weapons of mass destruction. Saddam Hussein, the Iraqi president, finally allowed the team to return in November 2002.

OPPOSITE: Armed guards outside the Moscow hospital at the center of a hostage crisis. In October 2002 about 50 armed Chechens claiming allegiance to the separatist movement in Chechnya stormed the hospital theater taking 850 hostages. Their demands included the withdrawal of Russian troops and an end to the second Chechen War, which had been raging for three years. Russian troops finally pumped chemicals into the ventilation system and raided the building. The gas killed at least 170 people and the move was widely condemned as being "heavy-handed."

2002

Stop the War Coalition

DON'T ATTACK IRAQ

www.stopwar.org.uk

Stop the War Coalition

DON'T ATTACK IRAQ

...out fir...

...ustice

Stop the War Coalition

NOT IN MY NAME

DON'T ATTACK IRAQ

STOP THIS BLOODY

ABOVE: The scenes in Kuta, on the island of Bali, after a car bomb detonated in the tourist area. The huge explosion ripped through two bars packed with foreign tourists, killing over 200 people and injuring hundreds of others. It was one of three bombs planted by Jemaah Islamiyah, a violent Islamic group. The perpetrators were caught and convicted and three men eventually faced the firing squad.

OPPOSITE: In a rally organized by the Stop the War Coalition and the Muslim Association of Britain anti-war protestors demonstrate outside Westminster in September 2002 to oppose a military strike on Iraq. Prime Minister Tony Blair had just set out the case for war and an estimated 400,000 people joined the peaceful protest.

2002

ABOVE: *Pop Idol* winner Will Young (right) and runner-up Gareth Gates. Although Gates came second in the show he was rapidly signed to the BMG label by Simon Cowell and his first single "Unchained Melody" went straight into the charts at number one. The pair recorded a cover version of "The Long and Winding Road" together which also peaked at number one.

OPPOSITE: Liam Gillick's *Coats of Asbestos Spangled with Mica* was shortlisted for the 2002 Turner Prize and went on show at Tate Britain in London along with the work of three other finalists. The prize was won by Keith Tyson, an artist noted for his painting series and installations.

ABOVE: Abu Hamza al-Masri, the imam at Finsbury Park Mosque, north London, joined Muslims gathering outside the mosque where a controversial conference entitled "September 11—A Towering Day in History" was due to take place. Some of the most radical Muslim clerics in Britain were engaged to speak at the event organized by the fundamental Islamic group Al-Muhajiroun. At the conference al-Masri established the Islamic Council of Britain to try to introduce Sharia law into the country. He was eventually jailed in 2004 for offences covered under the Terrorism Act 2000.

OPPOSITE: Jean-Marie Le Pen, presidential candidate and leader of the National Front party in France, speaks at a press conference at the party headquarters in Paris. He had run in three previous elections without any success, but in 2002 he secured enough votes in the first round to go through to the second. Over one million people rallied in the streets in protest and in the second round he was convincingly defeated, with Jacques Chirac claiming 82 percent of the votes.

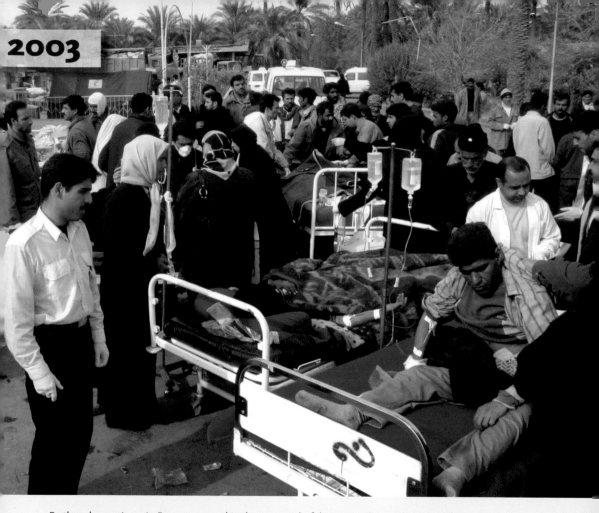

2003

Earthquake survivors in Bam are treated in the courtyard of the Imam Khomeini Hospital for fear of the building collapsing in aftershocks. The magnitude 6.5 earthquake struck the ancient Iranian city in the early hours of the morning while most of the city's residents were still in bed. Many of the city's poorly built mud-brick buildings collapsed during the earthquake, leading to a particularly high death toll.

Children attend ballet lessons wearing surgical masks to protect themselves from SARS, Severe Acute Respiratory Syndrome, in Hong Kong. The first cases of SARS emerged in southern China in November 2002, and by the spring of 2003 it had spread to more than twenty countries worldwide. More than 700 people died during the epidemic, mostly in China and Southeast Asia, but also in Canada, where there was a significant outbreak in the Toronto area.

2003

LEFT: The US space shuttle *Columbia* pictured inside the orbiter processing facility is readied for mission STS-107. The crew of six men and one woman, including Ilan Ramon, the first Israeli astronaut, lifted off from the Kennedy Space Center in January 2003.

OPPOSITE: A month after the launch, *Columbia* disintegrated as it re-entered the earth's atmosphere. Subsequent investigations revealed that during the launch a piece of foam had broken off the external tank and after striking the shuttle had damaged the thermal protection system designed to protect the craft from the heat generated during re-entry. The crew were killed instantly.

2003

ABOVE: Damien Hirst's "Away From the Flock" featured a lamb preserved in formaldehyde exhibited in a steel and glass case. Much of Hirst's early work was influenced by death and this became a central theme. In 1995 he won the Turner prize with "Mother and Child, Divided"—a bisection of a cow and calf, again presented in a preserved state.

OPPOSITE: "Zobop" by Jim Lambie was exhibited at Tate Modern in London. Lambie installed a psychedelic piece using multi-colored vinyl tape. He frequently used throwaway objects from everyday life in his work, including safety pins and plastic bags.

ABOVE: A police cordon blocks access to Wangford Road while the jury in the Soham murder trial visit the site where the bodies of Jessica Chapman and Holly Wells were discovered. The ten-year-old friends were murdered by school caretaker Ian Huntley after he had lured them into his house. The jury found him guilty of both murders and sentenced him to life in prison. His girlfriend, Maxine Carr, who was away at the time of the murders, was sentenced to almost four years in prison for perverting the course of justice.

OPPOSITE: Floral tributes are laid at the main Serbian government building in Belgrade following the assassination of Prime Minister, Zoran Djindjic. Djindjic's attempts to combat organized crime in Serbia earned him many enemies and he faced a number of attempts on his life. On March 12, his adversaries succeeded; he was shot by a sniper while walking toward the government building to meet Sweden's foreign minister, Anna Lindh.

Зоки
ОРАНЕ,
НЕДОСТИЖНИ,
НЕПРЕВАЗИЂЕНИ, ЗОРАНЕ,
ЈЕДИНСТВЕНИ
ХОЋЕ ЛИ ИКАДА
СРБИЈИ ДА СВАНЕ?!

RIGHT: Justin Timberlake teamed up with Christina Aguilera for a tour of the US and Canada between June and September 2003. The former NSYNC lead singer released his debut solo album *Justified* in 2002, with hits "Cry Me a River," "Like I Love You," and "Rock Your Body" storming music charts across the world.

OPPOSITE: Paul McCartney on his Back in the World tour. Between March and June the former Beatle toured thirteen European countries, culminating in a homecoming show in Liverpool.

2003

ABOVE: Thierry Henry celebrates as the final whistle is blown in the FA Cup final. Arsenal defeated Southampton 1-0 to retain the trophy. The fixture took place at the Millennium Stadium in Cardiff while the new Wembley stadium was being built.

OPPOSITE: The UK's national stadium at Wembley is demolished to make way for a new 90,000-seater facility. Many sports fans lobbied in vain for the iconic towers to be retained, but they were knocked down in favor of a grand arch that sweeps high above the new stadium.

2003

LEFT: A lifesize sculpture of a fire-eater by David Mach at the Royal College of Art's summer exhibition in London.

OPPOSITE: The redeveloped Bull Ring shopping center opened its doors in September 2003 amid widespread debate over whether the futuristic design was appropriate for central Birmingham, England.

RIGHT: Olafur Eliasson's The Weather Project encouraged people to reflect on their relationship with the weather during its stint in the Turbine Hall of the Tate Modern in London.

OPPOSITE: Magician David Blaine challenged himself to live in a perspex box above the River Thames for 44 days without food in September 2003. Spectators tried to tempt Blaine to break his fast by pelting the box with food, but he succeeded and emerged from the box in mid-October having lost a quarter of his body weight.

2003

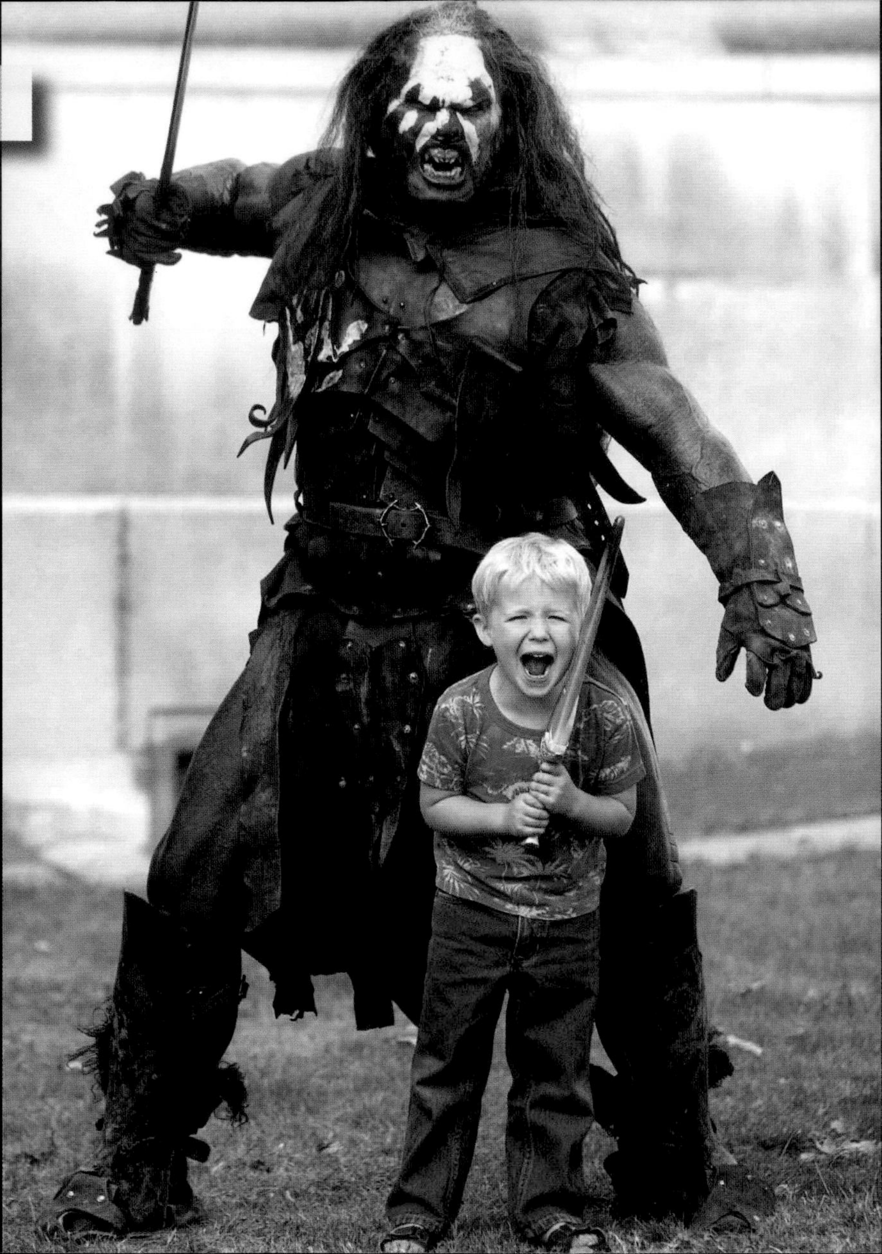

ABOVE: Tiger Woods practices for the 2003 British Open at the Royal St. George Club in Sandwich, Kent. Ben Curtis from Ohio won the competition by one stroke over Vijay Singh and Thomas Bjorn. Woods tied fourth with Davis Love III.

OPPOSITE: An Uruk-hai enlists a young apprentice while promoting the third instalment of the epic *Lord of the Rings* movie trilogy. *The Return of the King* hit cinemas in 2003 and scooped the Best Picture award at the Oscars the following year.

2003

Crowds gather to watch as the last ever Concorde flight lands at Heathrow airport. British Airways and Air France decided to retire their supersonic airliner fleets because they were not proving to be cost effective. Passenger numbers had sharply declined following the September 11 terrorist attacks and a deadly crash in Paris in July 2000.

The Rolling Stones on stage at the Harbour Fest in Hong Kong. The performance ended the Licks tour, during which the band delivered more than one hundred concerts across the world between September 2002 and November 2003. Originally the Hong Kong dates were scheduled for mid-tour, but were canceled as a result of the SARS epidemic.

2003

ABOVE: Images projected onto the Tate Britain promote the forthcoming exhibition "Pre Raphaelite Vision: Truth to Nature"—a study of the paintings dating back to the mid-nineteenth century examined how the artists were inspired by the scientific and religious beliefs of their day.

OPPOSITE: Brazilian Elaine Davidson, the Guinness world record holder for the woman with the greatest number of body piercings (1903) joins Britain's Stephen Taylor, the man with the longest tongue (3.7 inches), to mark the release of the 100th millionth copy of the *Guiness World Record* books.

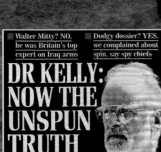

■ Walter Mitty? NO, he was Britain's top expert on Iraq arms   ■ Dodgy dossier? YES, we complained about spin, say spy chiefs

DR KELLY: NOW THE UNSPUN TRUTH EMERGES

DRAMATIC new evidence over the death of Dr David Kelly put Tony Blair's credibility on the line last night.

The first day of Lord Hutton's inquiry heaped blame on the Government over the Prime Minister's dossier telling the case for war against Iraq.

These key revelations unfolded as police revealed how "level of stress" in the civil servant's voice might have led him to take his own life.

RIGHT: Politician Clare Short's credibility was compromised after she backed away from her threat to quit the Cabinet over the Iraq war after she made a scathing attack on Tony Blair. The International Development Secretary reconsidered her decision and announced that she planned to stay on to help rebuild Iraq after the war. She said she had decided that quitting would be "cowardly" as she would be unable to help solve the problems ahead.

OPPOSITE: Police discover the body of Dr. David Kelly, a UK government weapons expert who had worked in Iraq during the 1990s. Dr. Kelly told a BBC journalist that the government had "sexed up" the case for war against Iraq. It quickly emerged that Dr. Kelly was the source of the quote and he found himself at the center of an international scandal. Unable to cope with the pressure, Dr. Kelly committed suicide in a field near his home in Oxford.

2003

OPPOSITE: US Army Black Hawk helicopters moved into Iraq during the opening stages of the invasion. In the early hours of the morning of March 20, 2003 explosions were heard in Baghdad as troops simultaneously crossed the border into Iraq. Within three weeks the military government had collapsed and the capital city of Baghdad captured.

ABOVE: Thousands of demonstrators take to the streets to protest against a state visit to London by American President, George W. Bush. Across the world many were opposed to the war in Iraq and as a consequence began to unite in protest. On February 15 and the following day, rallies were organized in over 800 cities, with the largest in Rome involving an estimated three million people.

2003

ABOVE: Iraq's Planning Ministry on the Tigris River in Baghdad is hit by a US missile on the opening day of the invasion. Thousands of bombs were aimed at sites linked to Saddam's regime in a campaign of "shock and awe," designed to soften up resistance to the ground troops crossing the Kuwaiti border in the south.

OPPOSITE: A US soldier carries a young girl to safety after insurgents attacked a US convoy. An estimated 7,500 civilians lost their lives during the invasion and over four million Iraqis have since fled from their homes and taken up refugee status. Half of these have left the country while the rest have been displaced internally.

2003

ABOVE: US General James Conway addresses the allied British troops in Kuwait. The invasion force had been largely made up from US and British troops as other super powers including France, Russia, and Germany had refused to offer their support.

2003

ABOVE: A British soldier with the Seventh Armored Division walks past ruined buildings in Mushirij, a village amid the oil fields west of Basra. British forces had battled their way toward Basra, Iraq's second-largest city, and after two weeks of fierce resistance were able to enter the town.

OPPOSITE: As coalition troops head north they pass thousands of refugees fleeing the bombing of Basra. The city had been left without water and refugees pleaded with coalition troops for a drink. Iraqi troops had been cleared from the port of Umm Qasr and soon ships carrying humanitarian aid were able to dock.

ABOVE: England celebrate after defeating Australia 20–17 to win the Rugby World Cup after a nail-biting final that went down to the last minutes of extra time. Captained by Martin Johnson and led by head coach Clive Woodward, the team returned home to join a celebratory parade through the streets of London before meeting the Queen at Buckingham Palace.

OPPOSITE: Johnny Wilkinson prepares to take a penalty during the final. Wilkinson, who played for Newcastle Falcons, took a drop goal 26 seconds before the final whistle, securing a victory for the national team. It was the first time England had won the Rugby World Cup and Wilkinson emerged as the tournament's leading points scorer. That year he was named BBC Sports Personality of the Year.

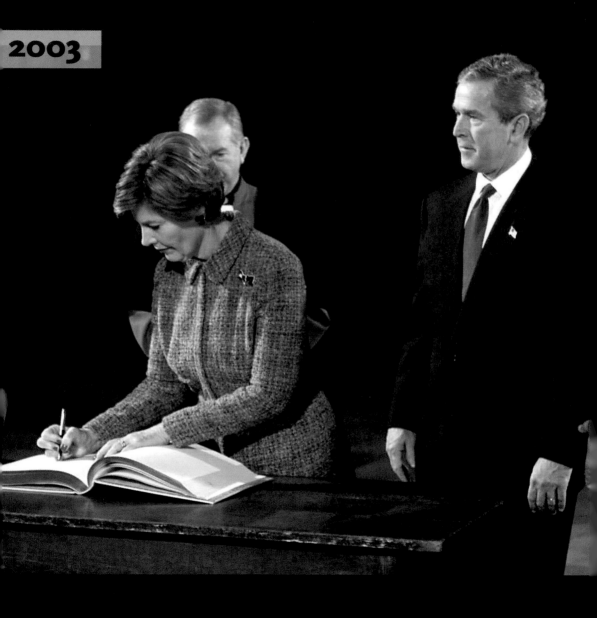
2003

ABOVE: Rescue workers search cars in Paso Robles, California, in the aftermath of the San Simeon earthquake on December 22, 2003 which struck 25 miles Northwest of Paso Robles. The quake registered a magnitude 6.6 on the Richter Scale.

OPPOSITE: George Bush pictured during the ceremony of the laying of the wreath on the tomb of the unknown soldier. The important issues in the Middle East, such as security and the lack of WMDs provided the agenda for the election campaign that would begin in earnest the following year. During his campaign, Bush's platform would change little from that of the 2000 election, although he added several claims of success in fighting the war on terror and preventing another 9/11-style attack.

In February, in the run-up to local government and European Parliament elections Oliver Letwin presented the Conservative Party's public spending proposals to the UK electorate. In a photo call, Conservative Party Leader Michael Howard and Oliver Letwin are pictured walking through a hall filled with 511 cardboard cut-out, derby-hatted faceless bureaucrats; the Conservatives say 511 was the average weekly increase in the number of staff employed in government last year and have pledged to freeze recruitment if they win the next UK general election.

Thousands of Haitian demonstrators run through the streets of downtown Port-au-Prince in late February, after hearing that Haitian President Jean Bertrand Aristide had fled the country. Early in the month the National Revolutionary Front for the Liberation of Haiti had seized control of the city of Gonaïves, and then proceeded down the coast, looting and burning until they were within a few miles of the presidential palace. President Aristide claimed the rebels were supported by the US and after he left Haiti on a US plane accompanied by US security personnel—he later claimed he had been abducted—1000 US Marines flew in as first representatives of a UN peacekeeping force.

RIGHT: The 2004 Cheltenham Gold Cup on March 18 was won by Jim Culloty on Best Mate; it was the third time they had won the race and Best Mate had became one of the most loved horses in British racing. When the horse died during a race at Exeter the following year, it made headline news.

OPPOSITE: In a simultaneous launch in New York, London, and Sydney in March, Speedo unveiled its newest and most extensively tested swimsuit ever, the Speedo Fastskin FSII. It had taken nearly four years of research to develop, in conjunction with a computational fluid dynamics engineer and software designer, the *Matrix* and *Spiderman* movie modeling company Cyber FX, and the resident shark expert at the Natural History Museum in London. Modeled here by members of Britain's 2004 Olympic team, the new body suit mimicked a shark's skin to reduce the body's friction in the water.

2004

ABOVE: David Moran, Kate Ashfield, Simon Pegg and Lucy Davis in a scene from *Shaun of the Dead*, which was directed by Edgar Wright and released in April 2004. The "romantic zombie comedy" film was both a critical and commercial success, earning US$3.3 million in its first weekend in the US despite a limited release. Time magazine later named it as one of the 25 best horror films.

OPPOSITE: The Trojan horse in a scene from the all-action film *Troy*, which starred Brad Pitt, and opened on May 14, 2004 in the United States It was one of the most expensive films ever made, costing more than $185 million, but made more than $497 million worldwide —taking it well into the top 100 top box-office hits of all time.

2004

ABOVE: In the Euro 2004 Group B match between France and England on June 13, England player Frank Lampard celebrates his goal, the first of the match, with 18-year-old rising star Wayne Rooney. However, France went on to score twice in injury time, winning the game 2–1. Both England and title-holders France qualified from the Group, but were both knocked out in the quarter-finals.

OPPOSITE: The Sugarbabes (from left: Mutya Buena, Heidi Range, and Keisha Buchanan) raise glasses of champagne to mark the first-ever triple rollover in the UK national lottery on May 29. The jackpot of more than £22 million was shared between six winning tickets.

2004

RIGHT: Top seed Roger Federer at the point of victory over Andy Roddick in the Wimbledon men's final on July 3. He won the match 6-2, 7-6 (7-2), 6-4, taking the title for the second consecutive year.

OPPOSITE: Maria Sharapova leaps across court to smash a forehand return back to number five seed Lindsay Davenport in their semi-final match at the Wimbledon Tennis Championships in London on July 1. The 17-year-old Sharapova beat former champion Davenport 2-6 7-6 6-1 to become the second-youngest Wimbledon finalist since tennis became a professional

2004

ABOVE: Madonna demonstrates amazing flexibility as she performs during the opening segment of her show during her Re-Invention world tour. The opening section featured some of her big hits, such as "Material Girl," "Vogue," and "Frozen". Tickets for all the shows in both the US and Europe were sold out as soon as they went on sale.

OPPOSITE: Singer-songwriter Alanis Morissette performing at the Party in the Park, a massive outdoor concert held on July 11 in Hyde Park in London to raise money for The Prince's Trust, which helps disadvantaged young people. More than 100,000 fans turned out but it was the last time the concert was held; the following year it was canceled because of a clash in dates with Live 8, and in 2006 the sponsors, London radio station Capital FM, pulled out.

ABOVE: The marching drum corps reflected in the still waters of a lake created by flooding the floor at the center of the stadium, during the opening ceremony of the 2004 Olympics in Athens on August 13. The widely praised opening event had been designed by avant-garde choreographer Dimitris Papaioannou.

OPPOSITE: The British team—Matthew Pinsent, Ed Coode, James Cracknell, and Steve Williams—after winning the men's coxless four gold medal at the Olympic Games in August. In a dramatic race that was very closely fought right to the very end, they had surged across the line at the final moment to beat the world champion Canadian crew. This was Pinsent's fourth consecutive Olympic gold medal.

RIGHT: Australia's Ian Thorpe celebrates his sensational victory after beating defending champion Pieter van den Hoogenband (Netherlands) to take the gold in the men's 200 meters freestyle at the Olympic Games on August 16. The "race of the century" pitted the four fastest male swimmers in history against each other: Thorpe, van den Hoogenband, Grant Hackett (Australia, the former world recordholder) and US teenage phenomenon Michael Phelps, who took the bronze.

OPPOSITE: Michael Phelps also took six gold medals at the Games – 100 meters butterfly, 200 meters butterfly, 200 meters individual medley, 400 meters individual medley, 4 x 200 meters freestyle relay, and 4 x 100 meters medley relay – as well as another bronze for the 4 x 100 meters freestyle relay. In the process he set two new world records, with a time of 4:08:26 in the 400 meters individual medley and 3:30:68 in the 100 meters medley relay.

2004

During the men's 1 kilometer time trial—a power sprinting event in which the rider must cover one kilometer (four laps) as fast as possible from a standing start—at the 2004 Olympics the world record was broken four times, the last time by Britain's Chris Hoy. Hoy took the gold to retain the title won by Jason Queally in Sydney in 2000.

OPPOSITE: In the finishing straight of the women's 800 meters at the Olympics, Britain's Kelly Holmes fights past Jolanda Cepnak (Slovenia), Hasna Benhassi (Morocco), reigning champion Maria Mutola (Mozambique), Tatyana Andrianova (Russia), and Jearl Miles Clark (USA) to take the gold. Holmes had only decided to enter the 800 meters at the last moment.

RIGHT: Holmes threw her arms wide with a big smile as she crossed the line, although she said later that she had to see the replay twice to be sure she had won. She also won the gold in the 1500 meters, making her the most successful UK athlete of recent years.

2004

ABOVE: Fans reach out to congratulate newcomer Todd Hamilton (USA) after his surprise play-off win against the favorite Ernie Els (South Africa) in the Open Golf Championship held in July at Royal Troon in Scotland. Hamilton only received his PGA Tour card the previous December, but had won the Honda Classic earlier in the year.

OPPOSITE: Cuba's Mario Cesar Kindelán Mesa (right) lands a punch on Britain's Amir Khan (left) during the Lightweight (60 kilogram) finals bout at the Olympic Games on August 29. Kindelán, who is widely considered to be one of the greatest amateur boxers the world has ever seen, went on to win the gold—as he had at Sydney in the 2000 Olympics.

RIGHT: Pro-hunt demonstrators outside the Houses of Parliament in London, while inside MPs vote on the Hunting Act 2004. The Act was passed, making hunting with dogs unlawful in England and Wales from February 2005. Fox-hunting in particular was a controversial issue in the UK: supporters claimed it was an essential part of rural life, important for conservation and pest control, while opponents thought it was cruel and unnecessary, and that more efficient methods of controlling the fox population could be employed.

OPPOSITE: Flowers on the gates of the Russian Embassy in London, in memory of those killed in Beslan School No.1. Heavily armed terrorists had stormed the school on September 1 during the opening day assembly and taken more than a thousand hostages, most of them children. They demanded an end to the Second Chechen War, but on the third day of the siege Russian troops stormed the school and the terrorists set off bombs in the gym, where most of the hostages were being held. In the explosions and following gun battle more than 350 people were killed—over half of them children.

2004

945-1990
SMALL GROUPS · BIG BOAT

ABOVE: Anti-war protesters and anti-globalization activists march through the streets of London to Trafalgar Square on October 17 to protest the US-led coalition's presence in Iraq. The rally was organized by the Stop the War Coalition and came at the end of the three-day European Social Forum, an event that opposes war, racism, and corporate power, which was dominated by debates on Iraq and the US presidential election.

OPPOSITE: In September, Hurricane Ivan caused widespread devastation over much of the Caribbean. Tropical Storm Ivan gathered strength as it moved west, and was categorized as a hurricane east of Tobago. Within days it had reached Category 5 on the Saffir-Simpson Hurricane Scale—the highest level possible—and at its peak extended for more than 265,000 square miles. It caused more than $13 billions' worth of damage to property and led to more than 120 deaths.

2004

Johnny Damon of the Boston Red Sox hits an RBI single in the third inning against the St. Louis Cardinals during game one of the World Series on October 23, 2004 at Fenway Park in Boston, Massachusetts. In this the 100th World Series, the Red Sox defeated the Cardinals four games to none in the best-of-seven. A home run by Damon in the first inning won game four for the Red Sox to secure the Series.

2004

OPPOSITE: Ukrainians attend a mass rally in support of opposition leader Viktor Yushchenko. In recent presidential elections in the Ukraine a second round of voting had finally led to a three percent margin of victory for Prime Minister Yanukovych, but there had been widespread allegations of election fraud. After 13 days of protests by citizens in Ukraine and around the world, the elections were run again at the end of December, giving Yushchenko 52 percent of the vote.

RIGHT: In December, the UK government announced a tough new approach to the growing trend of cars being illegally abandoned—in future, untaxed and unregistered vehicles would be removed from streets and public spaces and destroyed. Hazel Blears of the UK Home Office looks on as cars are crushed in a demonstration for the press.

2004

Queen Elizabeth II delivers her speech in the chamber of the House of Lords at the State Opening of Parliament in London on November 23. Key themes of the speech, which is written for her by the government and approved by the Cabinet, were homeland security and a reduction in crime.

2004

RIGHT: An impromptu candlelight vigil at the Atocha railway station, in memory of those killed in the terrorist bomb attacks in Madrid. On March 11, a series of coordinated bombings on the commuter train system had killed nearly 200 people and injured around 1,500. Blame was laid on an al-Qaeda-inspired terrorist group, although a direct connection with al-Qaeda could not be established.

OPPOSITE: The former President of South Africa, Nelson Mandela, smiles and waves as he leaves 10 Downing Street with Britain's Prime Minister Tony Blair on November 26. The two had met to discuss Blair's personal project to spearhead development activities in Africa during 2005, when Britain would hold the rotating presidencies of both the European Union and the Group of Eight (G8) industrialized nations' club.

2004

LEFT: US President George W. Bush at the Arromanches International Ceremony for the 60th anniversary of the D-day landings in June. He was one of 17 heads of state present at the ceremony, including Her Majesty Queen Elizabeth II. Veterans marched past the leaders under sunny skies to the strains of the theme music for the D-day film *The Longest Day*. Most of the Allied troops killed on D-day were American, and after telling veterans that they would be honored "ever and always," President Bush added, "America would do it again for our friends."

OPPOSITE: D-day veterans reflect on lost comrades at Juno Beach on the 60th anniversary of the landings, and some of them collected pebbles from the sand as mementos.

ABOVE: Presiding Officer George Reid surveys the debating chamber of the brand-new Scottish Parliament building in Edinburgh, Scotland, on October 9, before the very first royal opening to be held there. The Scottish Parliament had devolved from Westminster in 1999, but until then had been housed in temporary accommodation in the General Assembly Hall of the Church of Scotland.

OPPOSITE: Hilary Swank and Clint Eastwood in a scene from *Million Dollar Baby*, which was first released in December 2004 in the US and went on to win four Oscars—including Best Motion Picture of the Year—at the 2005 Academy Awards. Hilary Swank starred as a hillbilly woman who scrimps and scrapes to pay for professional boxing lessons at a gym owned by Eastwood.

2004

● CASUALTY TOLL COULD HIT 165,000 ● BRITISH PUBLIC RAISES £40m

NIGHTMARE

Desperate race against time to get aid to those facing death from disease and starvation

FULL REPORTS: PAGES 2-7

LEFT AND OPPOSITE: The remains of the city of Banda Aceh, on the island of Sumatra, which was almost completely destroyed by a tsunami on December 26. That day the second-biggest earthquake in recorded history ripped open the seafloor off the coast of northwest Sumatra, unleashing the devastating tsunami that in some places was more than 60 feet high. It traveled thousands of miles across the Indian Ocean, taking the lives of more than 200,000 people in countries as far apart as Indonesia, the Maldives, Sri Lanka, and Somalia. In the aftermath, millions struggled to find food and clean water and the world mobilized for the biggest relief efforts in history.

ABOVE: Front page of the London *Evening Standard* on December 31. The photograph shows an Indonesian woman covering her nose as she walks past a bridge filled with hundreds of corpses and debris in Banda Aceh.

ABOVE: Volunteers search desperately for bodies amongst the wreckage on the island of Sumatra in Indonesia following the tsunami that struck on December 26, 2004. Most places had little or no warning and communities were devastated. Over $7 billion of worldwide humanitarian aid was swiftly contributed.

OPPOSITE: Lebanese mourners carry the portrait of their former Prime Minister Rafic al-Hariri during his funeral procession in Beirut in February 2005. Hariri had been assassinated, along with 21 others, by an explosive device when his motorcade was traveling through the city. Tens of thousands joined the procession, many chanting anti-Syrian slogans as they believed Damascus was responsible for the bombing. The investigation into his death is still ongoing.

ABOVE: A sea of opposition protestors, estimated at over one million, gathered in central Beirut in March 2005. They had answered a call for a massive protest to demand the full withdrawal of Syrian troops and intelligence agents. The demonstration was held exactly a month after the death of Rafic al-Hariri and its organizers also demanded a a full investigation into his death and the resignation of senior security officials.

OPPOSITE: Beyoncé (right), David Beckham, and Jennifer Lopez at the world premiere of the new Pepsi television advert. A few days earlier Beckham's wife Victoria had given birth to their third son Cruz in a Madrid hospital, a brother for Brooklyn and Romeo. Beckham had joined Real Madrid for £25 million in July 2003 and the team won La Liga (the premier division) in 2007. That year it was announced Beckham would be moving to Los Angeles Galaxy.

2005

Steven Gerrard, the Liverpool captain, holds the UEFA Champions League trophy aloft following victory over AC Milan at the Olympic Stadium in Istanbul. Liverpool scored three goals in six minutes to level the game at 3–3. The scores remained the same at the end of extra time and a penalty shootout was required to decide the champions. Shevchenko, who had scored the winning penalty for Milan in 2003, hit his spot kick straight down the middle of the goal and Dudek blocked with his left hand to give Liverpool a 3–2 victory on penalties.

Daily Mail

PASSING OF THE POPE

As death drew close he raised his right hand as if blessing an unseen crowd and whispered his last word:

AMEN

ABOVE: Cardinals bless the coffin of Pope John Paul II during his funeral mass in St. Peter's Square at the Vatican in April 2005. The Polish-born Supreme Pontiff had served for twenty-seven years and the service was attended by the largest gathering of statesmen in history including George Bush, Jacques Chirac, Prince Charles, Tony Blair and King Juan Carlos I. His body was interred in the Tomb of the Popes.

RIGHT: The front page of the *Daily Mail* with the headline "Amen" showed a picture of Pope John Paul lying in state.

ABOVE: Cardinal Joseph Ratzinger of Germany was elected by the conclave 11 days after the funeral and took the name of Pope Benedict XVI. A strong defender of the Catholic doctrine and values, he has revived a number of traditions and focused on the need for the return to basic Christian ethics.

LEFT: White smoke pouring from the chimney of the Sistine Chapel indicated to the waiting crowds that the conclave had chosen the next Pope.

2005

Prince Charles, Prince of Wales, married Camilla Parker Bowles in a civil ceremony at the Guildhall in Windsor on April 9, 2005. The marriage was followed by a blessing at St. George's Chapel, led by the Archbishop of Canterbury, and a reception at Windsor Castle. After the union Camilla became HRH, Duchess of Cornwall.

Prince Harry, Prince William, and their cousin Zara Phillips lead the wedding party as they emerge from the Guildhall. This was the first time a member of the royal family had been married in a civil ceremony, chosen because both parties had previously been divorced.

2005

RIGHT: Bruce Forsyth and Tess Daly, hosts of BBC's *Strictly Come Dancing*, are pictured here promoting a lottery. The show that combined professional and celebrity dancers was an instant hit with viewers and the format was picked up by broadcasters across the world, spawning *Dancing with the Stars* in the US. In the UK newsreader Natasha Kaplinsky with professional partner Brendan Cole won the first series and in the US Kelly Monaco was the first winner.

OPPOSITE: Imperial stormtroopers from *Star Wars*, pictured as part of the events that took place to publicize the sixth film, *Star Wars: Episode III—Revenge of the Sith*. Written and directed by George Lucas, it starred Ewan McGregor and Hayden Christensen and broke box office records in the first week.

2005

OPPOSITE: Tom Cruise and his new love Katie Holmes pictured after the release of the movie *War of the Worlds*, which was adapted from the novel by H.G. Wells and directed by Stephen Spielberg. Cruise's film breakthrough came when he appeared in *Risky Business* which was soon followed by *Top Gun*, *The Color of Money*, and *Rain Man*. He has received three nominations for Academy Awards and won three Golden Globe awards. Cruise and Holmes were to marry in November 2006.

LEFT: A portrait of boxer Amir Khan, who won a silver medal in the lightweight category at the Athens Olympics.

2005

RIGHT: Michael Stipe of REM bows to the audience after a rendition of their classic single "Everybody Hurts" during their first full world tour for ten years.

OPPOSITE: Director and actor Sir Richard Attenborough hugs Juliet Mills during a memorial service for her father, Sir John Mills. Mills had died at the age of 97 after a career that spanned seven decades, making over 120 films, including many with director David Lean. Mills won an Academy Award for Best Supporting Actor in *Ryan's Daughter* and received a knighthood from the Queen in 1976.

2005

LEFT: Singer Robbie Williams performs in front of a crowd of over 200,000 at London's Live 8 concert in Hyde Park. It was just one of ten benefit concerts, initiated by Bob Geldof and Midge Ure, held in the G8 states and South Africa to support the Global Call for Action against Poverty. They were timed to coincide with the G8 summit at Gleneagles in Scotland. Other performers in London included Paul McCartney, Madonna, UB40, The Who, and Pink Floyd. In Philadelphia the lineup included Bon Jovi, Alicia Keys, Stevie Wonder, and Destiny's Child.

OPPOSITE: Mobile screens transmit Madonna's set throughout the park. The event, broadcast both on television and radio, eventually overran by three hours, finally finishing after midnight.

ABOVE: At 8:50 a.m. on Thursday, July 7, four bombs exploded in central London within 50 seconds of each other. The targets were a London bus and three subway stations. Intended to destroy lives and cause chaos during the morning rush hour, the devices killed 56 people and injured another 700.

OPPOSITE: Injured and dazed passengers escaped from Russell Street station onto the streets above. As the emergency services swung into action all rail journeys in the capital were suspended and roads became gridlocked. Buses were used to ferry the injured to hospital and armed soldiers were ordered onto the streets to protect key buildings.

2005

ABOVE: Emergency services outside Edgware Road station. The day before the capital had been celebrating having won the 2012 Olympic bid; less than twenty-fours later it was in mourning.

OPPOSITE: A man from Kuwait prays for the victims outside Edgware Road Station. Four Muslim suicide bombers, who were unknown to the authorities and gave no warning of the attacks, caused the explosions.

Tim Duncan of the San Antonio Spurs shoots against Ben Wallace of the Detroit Pistons in game seven of the 2005 NBA Finals on June 23, 2005 at the SBS Center in San Antonio, Texas. The Spurs won the series 4 games to 3 in the first NBA Finals to go to a game seven since 1994. This series was the first Finals to feature the previous two champions since the 1987 Finals.

2005

ABOVE: Hu Jintao, President of China, inspects a guard of honor at Horse Guards Parade during the official ceremonial welcome for his visit to London. However, the pomp was soon combined with protest when hundreds of demonstrators from the Free Tibet Campaign, who called for an end to the Chinese occupation of Tibet, packed into The Mall nearby to publicize their protest.

OPPOSITE: Activists battle with police in a field at Auchterarder after breaching a fence surrounding the G8 summit at Gleneagles. Tony Blair hosted the conference and the agenda included global climate change and the lack of economic development in Africa. G8 summits often attracted protests in various forms and many people wanted to highlight the Make Poverty History campaign. More than 200,000 people had marched through Edinburgh four days earlier in support of action.

2005

ABOVE: The day after Hurricane Katrina swept through the city of New Orleans over 80 percent of the city was left flooded after the local series of defenses failed. Eighteen hundred people lost their lives and the cost of damage to property was estimated at $100 billion.

OPPOSITE: Boats at a marina in the city were tossed together like toys. A state of emergency had been declared before the hurricane even reached land, mandatory evacuation of the city was

2005

RIGHT: Shane Warne of Australia (left) and England's Kevin Pietersen shake hands after Pietersen was out for 158 on the final day of the fifth Test match between England and Australia at The Oval cricket ground.

OPPOSITE: Michael Vaughan, the England captain, raises the Ashes into the air as the team celebrates winning the series 2-1 after the fifth test was drawn. It was the first time England had won the much-coveted trophy since 1987.

ABOVE: Professional ballroom dancer Anton Du Beke teaches two new students the basics of ballroom dancing. Following the success of the television program *Strictly Come Dancing* "formal" dancing took Britain by storm and many took up lessons. Du Beke has appeared in all the series of *Strictly Come Dancing* and professionally dances with fellow contestant Erin Boag.

OPPOSITE: (L–R) Louis Walsh, Sharon Osbourne, and Simon Cowell at the launch of ITV's second series of the talent competition *The X Factor*. It was eventually won by Shayne Ward who immediately signed a recording contract with Sony BMG and released the single "That's My Goal." The song shot to number one remaining there for four weeks and was given an Ivor Novello award for Best Selling Single.

2005

ABOVE: British Prime Minister, Tony Blair and Chancellor of the Exchequer, Gordon Brown. Blair won his third general election in 2005 but the previous year had announced that he would not take the party into a fourth election. Brown at a very early stage was a clear candidate to replace him as leader of the Labour Party.

OPPOSITE: The Prince of Wales and the Duchess of Cornwall met President George Bush and his wife Laura in Washington DC. The royal couple had embarked on a week-long tour of the country, their first official overseas tour since their marriage. They included time to visit Ground Zero to pay their respects to those killed in the September 11 attacks.

2005

LEFT: Buncefield oil storage depot in Hemel Hempstead, near London, ignited after a series of explosions at 6 a.m. on the morning of Sunday, December 12. Due to the atmospheric conditions the blast was heard up to 125 miles away and shockwaves were felt in a 30-mile radius. Several local buildings and cars were damaged but fortunately, because the accident occurred at such an early hour, no one was killed although several were injured or suffered breathing difficulties due to smoke particles in the atmosphere. Flames shot hundreds of feet into the air and it finally took 150 firefighters 36 hours to extinguish the blaze. Local residents were evacuated while schools and public buildings were closed for two days.

ABOVE: The front page of the *Daily Mail* graphically shows the extent of the smoke from the fire in a photograph taken in central London, over 20 miles from the scene.

ABOVE: Tourists view a solar eclipse in front of Apollo Temple in the Turkish Mediterranean coastal resort of Side, Turkey, Wednesday, March 29, 2006. The total solar eclipse began at sunrise on the eastern tip of Brazil, crossed the Atlantic and made landfall in Ghana, headed north across the Sahara, the eastern Mediterranean, Turkey and the Black Sea, and on into Central Asia, where it finally died out at sunset in Mongolia.

OPPOSITE: British Foreign Secretary Jack Straw and US Secretary of State Condoleezza Rice arrive at Pleckgate High School in Blackburn, Lancashire. Protesters heckled the US Secretary of State with chants of "how many children have you killed?" and "Condi Rice, terrorist." The two-day visit to the town by the world's most powerful woman was supposed to have been a personal triumph for her host, Blackburn MP Jack Straw. Instead the trip became a propaganda victory for opponents of the Iraq war. Dozens of children who were to have met Miss Rice in their assembly hall at the Blackburn school took the day off to voice their protest.

2006

OPPOSITE: A technician works on the 10-feet-tall holographic image of Richard Burton as it floats above the stage in front of a computer-generated backdrop of Martian invaders at Bray Film Studios, Berkshire. Two decades after his death, Burton will appear before an audience once again thanks to the wonders of digital technology in the stage version of *The War of the Worlds*, an adaptation by Jeff Wayne of his 1978 concept album which turned the sci-fi classic by H.G. Wells into a rock opera.

RIGHT: Singing star Dannii Minogue pictured at the launch of British Airways' one-way European ticket offer. BA cut its fares by up to 50 percent to more than 65 destinations across Europe in an attempt to win back passengers from its budget rivals. The first years of the new millennium were disastrous for the traditional large airlines—four of the six US legacy operators filed for Chapter 11 protection and set about major efficiency savings. BA and other major European airlines were forced to rethink their operations.

2006

Quarterback Ben Roethlisberger of the Pittsburgh Steelers passes the football against the Seattle Seahawks in Super Bowl XL at Ford Field in Detroit, Michigan, on February 5, 2006. The Steelers defeated the Seahawks 21–10. The Steelers became the second team after the 1985 New England Patriots to win three road playoff games to reach the Super Bowl.

2006

ABOVE: Film stars Tom Hanks and Audrey Tautou with movie director Ron Howard unveil the name of the new Eurostar Train, then, with other cast-members of the Hollywood blockbuster *The Da Vinci Code*, boarded the high-speed train heading for the Cannes Film Festival. On May 16, Eurostar set a new world record for the longest international non-stop journey—883 miles—with the cast of the film on board. It arrived in Cannes in time for the premiere of the film after a journey duration of 7 hours 25 minutes.

OPPOSITE: Pop-rock band McFly came to fame in 2004, taking their name from the protagonist family in the 1980s movie trilogy *Back to the Future*. In 2006 they had their own Hollywood experience when they appeared as themselves in *Just My Luck*, a movie starring Lindsay Lohan.

2006

OPPOSITE: Alecia Beth Moore—better known as Pink. In 2006 Pink released her fourth album *I'm Not Dead*, which gave her seven hit singles, one of which, "Stupid Girls" gained her both a Grammy nomination and MTV Award for Best Pop Video.

ABOVE: British girl vocal band the Sugababes looking suitably demure for The Prince's Trust 30th Anniversary concert. Prior to the show they met the royal party, apparently using a cellphone to record the encounter. Sadly the phone went missing soon after but the concert was a massive success, raising in the region of £3 million for the Trust.

The Cassini spacecraft launched from Cape Canaveral in 1997 on a mission to investigate the planet Saturn and its moon Titan. Here we see the small, battered moon, Epimetheus, and smog-enshrouded Titan, with Saturn's A and F rings stretching across the scene. Epimetheus is 72 miles across and giant Titan is 3,200 miles across. The image was taken in visible light with the Cassini spacecraft narrow-angle camera on April 28, 2006, at a distance of approximately 415,000 miles from Epimetheus and 1.1 million miles from Titan. Cassini's surface probe of the moon discovered giant lakes of liquid gas while a number of previously unknown moons were discovered during Cassini's orbit. The highly successful mission may have up to two extensions before its planned crash-landing on Saturn in 2017.

This image provided by NASA is a recent photo from the Cassini spacecraft showing the planet Saturn, and if you look very closely between its wing-like rings, upper left, a faint pinprick of light is visible. That tiny dot is Earth. The image is the second ever taken of our world from deep space. The first was captured by the Voyager spacecraft in 1990. This panoramic view was created by combining a total of 165 images taken by the Cassini wide-angle camera over nearly three hours on September 15, 2006. The mosaic images were acquired as the spacecraft drifted in the darkness of Saturn's shadow for about 12 hours, allowing a multitude of unique observations of the microscopic particles that compose Saturn's faint rings.

2006

ABOVE: Wolverine clasps Dr Jean Grey in a passionate but doomed embrace in the third film in the successful X-Men franchise, *X Men: The Last Stand*, directed by Brett Ratner. 2006 was a busy year for actor Hugh Jackman, who played Wolverine: he starred in *The Prestige*, cult movie *The Fountain*, and Woody Allen's *The Scoop*. Dutch actress Famke Janssen, who appeared as Jean Grey, is best known as the Bond villain Xenia Onatopp, who killed her victims by crushing them between her thighs, in the 1995 *GoldenEye*.

OPPOSITE: Take That on stage in Dublin on June 28, during their Ultimate tour. After reuniting for a TV documentary the band signed a new contract with Polydor Records for a reported £3 million. US girl band Pussycat Dolls were in support for the Dublin show while the Sugababes stepped in for the final five gigs of the tour. Take That's comeback album, *Beautiful World*, released in 2006, was a huge success.

ABOVE: Germany was the host country of the 2006 FIFA World Cup tournament held from June 9 to July 9. Qualifying games began in 2003, involving 198 teams, which eliminated all but 32 for the final competition. With satellite technology and improved screening, this was one of the most watched TV events of all time with over 25 billion viewers during the course of the competition. Here Australian football fans cheer on their team.

OPPOSITE: England striker Wayne Rooney gets a red card during the quarter-final game against Portugal at Gelsenkirchen, Germany. With the star out of the game and captain, David Beckham, substituted because of injury, England struggled for the rest of the match, eventually losing in the third penalty shoot-out of the tournament, resulting from the 0–0 score after overtime. Portugal went on to face France in the semi-final and were narrowly defeated after Zidane scored the only goal of the match from the penalty spot.

2006

ABOVE: The World Cup was marred by football violence; here fans clash in Stuttgart's central Schlosse Platz after the Germany v Sweden match which ended in a 2-2 draw. On the pitch, the number of cards issued to players exceeded previous competitions—345 yellow cards and 28 red cards.

OPPOSITE: Italian football fans bring traffic to a standstill as they celebrate their country's victory in the final of the World Cup 2006; Italy beat France 5–3 on penalties after the match ended 1–1. However, the most notorious incident of the tournament occurred during during extra time in the final when France midfielder Zinedine Zidane headbutted Marco Materazzi in response to the Italian's protracted verbal abuse. Although he was sent off for the incident Zidane was allowed to keep the Golden Ball award for being the best player of the 2006 competition.

RIGHT: Rock 'n' roll couple Pete Doherty and Kate Moss. Doherty, Babyshambles founder and lead singer, won the heart of top model Moss with his wide-eyed baby face and his bohemian persona. His substance-fueled lifestyle kept the singer in the courts and in the eye of the media. The couple met up at Kate Moss's 31st birthday party and embarked on a wild and public relationship which also broke down in the full glare of tabloid coverage.

OPPOSITE: Decked out in white, celebrity couple Girls Aloud singer Cheryl Tweedy and football star Ashley Cole launch the National Lottery Dream Number created in July 2006 to raise funds for the London 2012 Olympic Games. The pair married on July 15—the same day as the first Dream Number draw.

2006

OPPOSITE: The southern Beirut area of Musharachea, in the suburb of Dahiye, which bore the brunt of an Israeli attack on targets in Lebanon. This was part of the 34-day conflict called the July War that erupted when Hezbollah fired on an Israeli border patrol in Northern Israel on July 12. Israel's retaliation was fierce but the world watched a surprisingly strong response from Hezbollah. Ultimately it was Lebanese civilians that paid the highest price, both in death toll and in damage to the recovering infrastructure.

ABOVE: Bint Jbeil, Lebanon. After three weeks of ground battles between Hezbollah and Israeli forces, a 48-hour cease-fire allowed journalists and Red Cross officials to enter the town for the first time. Journalists and their drivers helped to evacuate some of the destitute and injured who were stranded in the town throughout the raging firefights and bombardments.

2006

OPPOSITE: Daniel Craig debuts as Agent 007 in the 21st Bond movie, *Casino Royale*. Craig's rugged physical presence and more brutal persona contrasted with the more refined and sophisticated Bond portrayed by Pierce Brosnan. Extreme physical stunts and an amusing homage to the classic *Dr. No* scene where Ursula Andress emerges from the ocean were just some of the touches that made *Casino Royale* a critical and financial success.

ABOVE: Richard Griffiths plays English teacher Douglas Hector opposite Dominic Cooper as Dakin in the award-winning movie *The History Boys*, directed by Nicholas Hytner and adapted by the playwright Alan Bennett from his own play. *The History Boys* stage production had a successful run at the National Theatre in London before transferring to Broadway where it opened to a spectacularly successful season in April 2006, running with extensions until October. The movie reunited the original stage cast with the director of the first stage production.

2006

OPPOSITE AND LEFT: November 2006 saw The Beatles firmly back to a peak of international popularity with the *Love* album. Producer George Martin and son Giles re-mixed previous Beatles classics with the support of Paul McCartney and Ringo Starr as well as Olivia Harrison and Yoko Ono. The album was an artistic achievement and a commercial coup—not just for the Beatles but also for the innovative entertainment troupe Cirque du Soleil who built a performance program on the music. Paul McCartney (left) also benefited from the wave of interest in the run-up to Christmas—in this picture fans line up to meet McCartney who was promoting his new album *Ecce Cor Meum* and his DVD *The Space Within Us.*

2006

ABOVE: The 2006 US Ryder Cup team pose at the K Club, County Kildare, Ireland. Although the US team included the three world-ranking players, Tiger Woods, Phil Mickelson, and Jim Furyk, they were unable to defend themselves against a convincing victory by the Europeans who beat them by 18^1/$_2$ to 9^1/$_2$ points, their third victory in a row and a repeat of the 2004 tournament score.

OPPOSITE: Australian captain Ricky Ponting celebrates his century during the afternoon of the first day of the 2006–07 Test Match Series between Australia and England in Brisbane, Australia. Ponting, named man of the match, almost made a double century, finally bowled at 196 runs by Matthew Hoggard. The series was dominated by the Australian side who won each of the five Test matches to regain the Ashes won by England in 2005.

LEFT: Tate Modern held a major exhibition of the work of Gilbert & George. Gilbert Proesch (seated) and George Passmore are part of a handful of artists who have become household names, their impeccably dressed figures instantly recognizable. *Gilbert & George: Major Exhibition* brought together a selection of pictures that spanned their 40-year career, the largest retrospective of any artist to be held at Tate Modern.

OPPOSITE: A retrospective Antony Gormley exhibition, *Blind Light*, which opened in May at the Hayward Gallery in London, included a massive sculpture project, *Event Horizon*, consisting of 31 life-size male bodies set on top of prominent London buildings. The sculptures were seen best when viewed from terraces at the gallery. Gormley's best-known work is *Angel of the North*, a steel sculpture 66 feet high with wings almost 180 feet across.

2007

ABOVE: US President George W. Bush and his wife Laura Bush pose with Pope Benedict XVI, at the Vatican on June 9. The President and the Pontiff had met privately; during his stay in Rome President Bush also met the Italian Premier Romano Prodi and former Premier and conservative leader Silvio Berlusconi.

OPPOSITE: US Vice-President Al Gore arriving in Dublin, where he was giving a speech on climate change. In October, he had been awarded the Nobel Peace Prize—jointly with the Intergovernmental Panel on Climate Change (IPCC)—for their efforts in spreading greater knowledge about global warming.

2007

LEFT: Tiger Woods during the second round of the 136th Open Championship, held at Carnoustie Golf Club, Scotland, in July.

ABOVE: During the British Open, American golfer Tiger Woods hit a ball that went into the crowd, knocking spectator Jennifer Wilson to the ground. She was struck on the head, causing a wound that needed two stitches. As paramedics tended to her, Woods walked over, knelt down to hold her hand and said: "I'm sorry. I'm so sorry. I can't believe that has happened." After completing the hole, he made amends by giving the woman the ball used in the game as well as a signed golf glove.

OPPOSITE: US President George W. Bush meets Marines during his visit to Al-Asad Air Base in Anbar Province, Iraq, in September 2007.

ABOVE: President Bush gestures during a news conference, in the Brady Press Room at the White House, Washington DC.

LEFT: South African icon Nelson Mandela at the unveiling of a statue of himself in Parliament Square, London, on August 29. The 9-feet-tall bronze sculpture took its place alongside other historical figures, such as Britain's Second World War leader Winston Churchill and 19th-century US President Abraham Lincoln.

OPPOSITE: There was a surprise for the fashion world at London Fashion Week in September, when American rock star Prince jumped up onto the catwalk to sing at Matthew Williamson's first London show in five years. At first the star had appeared to be there just to watch the show from the first row of the audience, but then his song "U Got The Look" began to play; his 10-minute performance had the audience on its feet cheering and applauding.

ABOVE: James McAvoy (Robbie) and Keira Knightley (Cecilia) in the dinner party scene from *Atonement*, which was released in September in the UK and December in the US. Based on the novel of the same name by Ian McEwan, and set mainly just before and during the Second World War, *Atonement* was one of the top films of 2007 and opened both the Venice and the Vancouver international film festivals. It featured strong performances, brilliant cinematography, and a unique score, as well as deft performances from McAvoy and Knightley and won numerous awards—although only one Oscar.

OPPOSITE: Javier Bardem as Anton Chigurh in a scene from the Coen brothers' film, *No Country for Old Men*, which was adapted from the novel of the same name by Cormac McCarthy. The centerpiece of the 45th annual New York Film Festival in September/October, the thriller also starred Tommy Lee Jones and Josh Brolin, and told of the violence and mayhem that ensue after a hunter stumbles upon some dead bodies, a stash of heroin, and more than $2 million in cash near the Rio Grande. *No Country for Old Men* was not only praised by the critics but also won four Oscars at the Academy Awards, as well as three British Academy of Film Awards.

The Meeting Place, a bronze statue by sculptor Paul Day, looms over St Pancras International railroad station. The statue, which is over 30 feet high and weighs over 4 tons, was commissioned by London and Continental Railways for the newly renovated station, which became the London terminus of the Eurostar from November 14.

A woman takes a closer look at *Shibboleth*, by Colombian artist Doris Salcedo. The giant crack in the floor, 550 feet long and over 3 feet deep in places, began as a hairline crack at the western end and zigzagged across the floor of the Turbine Hall at Tate Modern, London, becoming 10 inches across at its widest point.

2007

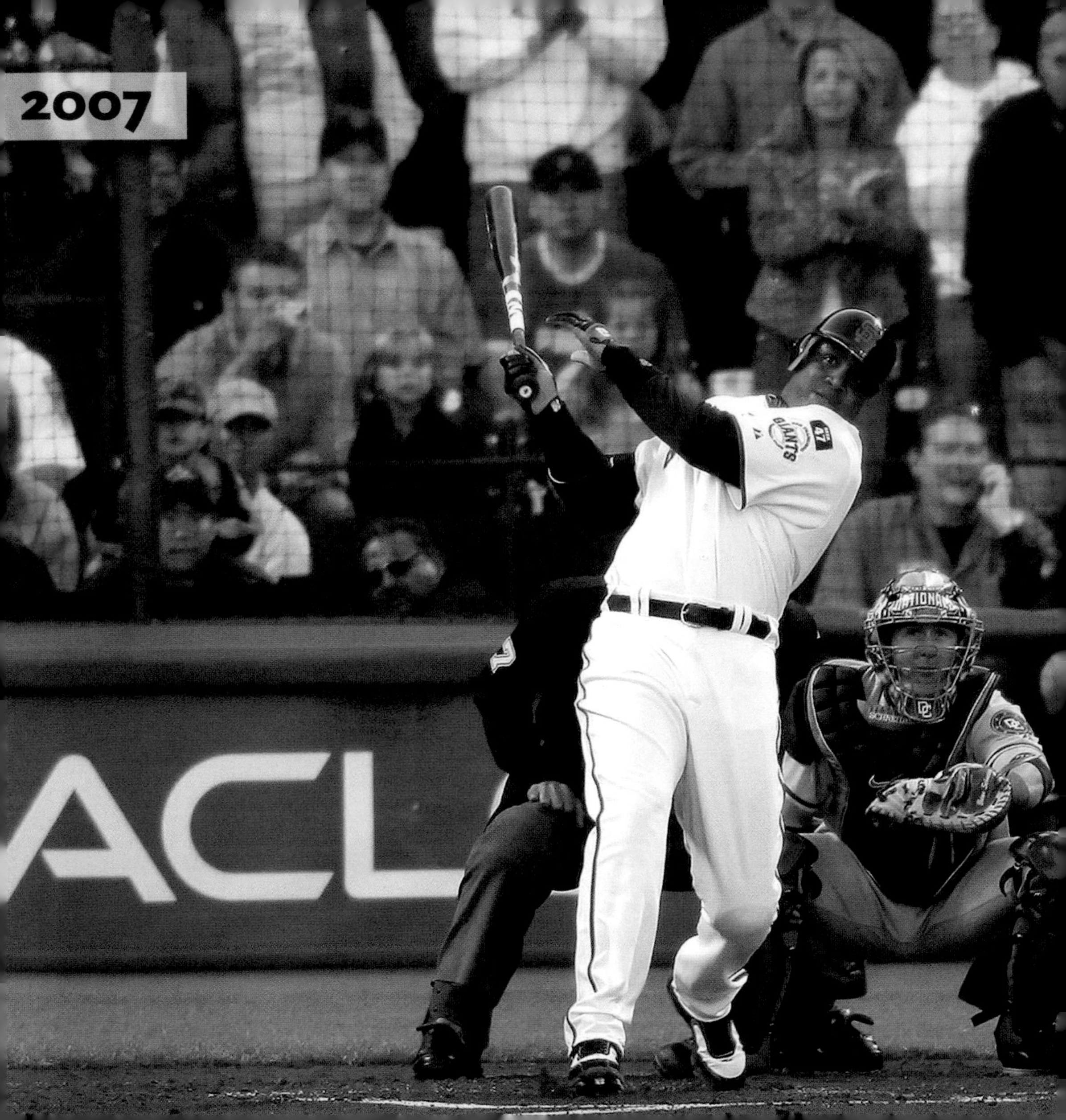

Barry Bonds of the San Francisco Giants swings at the pitch during the game against the Washington Nationals in San Francisco. With his 756th career home run, Barry Bonds surpassed Hank Aaron to become Major League Baseball all-time home run leader.

2007

LEFT: Irish Taoiseach Bertie Ahern with former US president Bill Clinton in Dublin in November. Mr Clinton had traveled to Ireland to raise funds for wife Hillary's campaign to be nominated as the Democratic presidential candidate; she was standing against Barack Obama and John Edwards. Mr Clinton attended a fundraising dinner at the home of Dublin lawyer and US citizen Brian Farren, which was organized by Irish-Americans, and had earlier been briefed on recent political progress in Northern Ireland. On June 7, 2008, Mrs Clinton suspended her campaign and endorsed Obama, who by that time was well in the lead in the primaries.

OPPOSITE: US President George W. Bush waves as he arrives to greet German Chancellor Angela Merkel on November 9. The chancellor had been invited to stay at the president's ranch in Crawford, Texas—an invitation reserved for close allies—where they aimed to discuss several international issues, including Iran's nuclear program, the Israeli-Palestinian peace process, and global warming.

2007

ABOVE: US President George W. Bush with Afghanistan's first democratically-elected President, Hamid Karzai, during their joint press conference on August 6 at Camp David, Maryland. Karzai's two-day visit to the presidential mountain retreat included discussions about the resurgence of the Taliban, although he was adamant that they presented no real threat to his government.

OPPOSITE: British Conservative Party Leader David Cameron at home in London with his wife Samantha. At the end of the Conservative Party conference in October, Cameron had challenged Labour Prime Minister Gordon Brown to call an immediate general election to "let the people decide." After the conference, The *Guardian* reported that the Conservatives had drawn level with Labour in popularity, but by December the collapse of Northern Rock bank and scandals about Labour's political donations had given the Conservatives an 11-point lead.

In the British Grand Prix on July 8, McLaren team driver Lewis Hamilton briefly lurched forward with the fuel hose attached to his car when he reacted too soon to the "lollipop" board being turned over. Hamilton led the race until lap 16, but was later forced to settle for third place, behind team-mate Fernando Alonso and winner Kimi Räikkönen, driving for Ferrari. Hamilton finished his first Formula One Championship in second place.

2007

RIGHT: Padraig Harrington with the claret jug trophy after winning the British Open Championship at Carnoustie on July 22. It was Harrington's first major triumph, and the first success by an Irishman in the Open since Fred Daly in 1947.

OPPOSITE: Private Ben Anderson of the British Army's Theatre Military Working Dogs Support Unit with his three-year-old black Labrador, Jack, at Basra International Airport compound. Jack inspects trucks coming into the compound, searching for hidden weapons or explosives, and is a vital part of the British Army's efforts to keep peace in the region. On September 3, British troops pulled out of Basra city and moved to a base at the airport, and on December 16 responsibility for the security of Basra province was handed over to the Iraqi authorities, four-and-a-half years after the invasion.

ABOVE: The Archbishop of Canterbury, Dr. Rowan Williams, speaking at the General Synod. In a speech in February he had suggested that there was a role for Sharia law in the UK, which had been widely interpreted as suggesting that Muslims should be allowed to live by Sharia as an alternative to being subject to the UK's civil laws. This had provoked an unprecedented and widespread chorus of condemnation and plunged the Church of England into crisis, with demands for the Archbishop to resign. He blamed himself for "unclarity," a misleading choice of words, and clumsiness, but refused to back down from his belief that there should be "additional choices" for Muslims under the law of the land.

OPPOSITE: American singer Madonna, with her daughter Lourdes and David Banda Mawali in her arms, at the Home of Hope Orphan Care Center in Mchinji, Malawi, in April. Madonna had met one-year-old David when she visited the orphanage the previous year, and decided she wanted to adopt him. Amidst accusations that she was "fast-tracking" the adoption—under Malawian law, prospective parents have to be resident in the country for 18 months before adoption can be approved—she had gained an interim adoption order allowing her to take David back to the UK. The adoption was finalized in May 2008.

2007

ABOVE: Former Pakistani Prime Minister Benazir Bhutto waves to supporters as she arrives at a local court in Larkana, on November 26 to submit her nomination papers for the forthcoming Pakistani general election. Bhutto had only recently returned to Pakistan from a self-imposed exile in Dubai.

OPPOSITE: Lighted candles and flowers are placed in front of a portrait in memory of Benazir Bhutto. On December 27, she was assassinated as she was leaving a Pakistan Peoples Party campaign rally in the city of Rawalpindi; she was traveling in a bullet-proof vehicle, but had stood up to wave to crowds through the open roof, and a lone gunman fired several shots while explosives were also detonated nearby, killing several bystanders. Bhutto was badly injured in the attack and was rushed to hospital, where she later died. There were conflicting reports and contradictions about the cause of death—some said a gunshot wound, others that she had suffered a serious head wound from the blast—and it has never been established who was responsible for the attack.

2008

Serbian riot police carry an injured colleague away during clashes with protesters in front of the US embassy in Belgrade, Serbia. On February 17 Kosovo had declared its independence from Serbia and the following day the US, Great Britain, and France had recognized the new Republic of Kosovo as an independent state, along with four other countries. Several thousand Serbs had gathered outside the US embassy to vent their anger at American backing for the breakaway province.

On March 17, Serb protesters clash with French NATO peacekeeping troops in the city of Kosovska Mitrovica, situated in the north of Kosovo. After the Kosovo War of 1999, the southern part of the city had become home mainly to ethnic Albanians, while the northern part held mainly ethnic Serbs. The unrest in March began after Serbs occupying a government building in an attempt to have their jobs reinstated were arrested by international police and transported away in UN vehicles. Other Serbs attacked the UN convoy and the violence quickly escalated across the city, leaving several dead and hundreds injured.

2008

ABOVE: Her Majesty Queen Elizabeth II meets Australian Prime Minister Kevin Rudd at Windsor Castle, Windsor on April 7. It was around this time that Rudd recommended the appointment of Quentin Bryce as the first female Governor-General of Australia. The decision to do so was announced on April 13, and was generally well received.

OPPOSITE: Kenyan Wildlife Service wardens in Tsavo East National Park patrol for poachers, carrying Kalashnikov 101 guns. In July, China—the center of the illegal ivory trade—became a licensed buyer of ivory, despite opposition from several African countries. Later in 2008, the UN Convention for International Trade in Endangered Species (CITES) temporarily lifted a ban on ivory sales so existing stockpiles—or ivory from elephants that died naturally—could generate much-needed income for Africa. Conservationists warned of an increase in poaching in both Africa and Asia as a result.

2008

Chelsea's Frank Lampard sends the ball crashing into the net to score the 1–1 equalizer in the Chelsea v Manchester United final of the 2007–08 UEFA Champions League on May 21. The match was played at the Luzhniki Stadium in Moscow—the first time it had been held in Russia, and it was also the first time that Chelsea (owned by Russian businessman Roman Abramovich) had reached the final.

Manchester United players hold aloft the European Cup in triumph, after winning 6–5 on penalties against Chelsea. It was the first time in the history of the competition that both teams in the UEFA Champions League final had been English, and only the third time that both were from the same country. At full time in the thrilling contest the score stood at 1–1, and even after extra time in pouring rain there were no more goals—until a dramatic shootout sealed United's third triumph.

The win was particularly poignant for Manchester United, as 2008 was the 50th anniversary of the Munich air disaster in 1958, in which they lost eight players and three staff members, and the 40th anniversary of their first Cup win in 1968. Sir Bobby Charlton, who survived the Munich disaster and went on to score twice in the 1968 European Cup Final win against SL Benfica, led the United players up the stairs at the Luzhniki Stadium to collect the Cup.

ABOVE: English-Swedish alternative rock band Razorlight entertain a selected audience during a concert in support of The Big Ask, a campaign by Friends of the Earth calling for a new climate change law to tackle the rise in the emission of carbon dioxide. On October 28, British MPs voted in favor of a Climate Change Law that will cut greenhouse gases by 80 percent by 2050 and includes all UK emissions—the first law of its kind anywhere in the world.

OPPOSITE: On July 23, Madame Tussauds in London unveiled their new waxwork of Grammy Award-winning singer Amy Winehouse, dressed in the same outfit that the real Amy wore to the Brit awards—a thigh-skimming yellow mini-dress teamed with black high heels. The singer's parents, Mitch and Janis, said the waxwork of their 24-year-old daughter was an "absolutely incredible" likeness. The singer had been hitting the headlines over the last few months, having performed at the recent Nelson Mandela concert in London and the Glastonbury Festival.

2008

ABOVE: Armed Georgian police in Gori, Georgia. In early August, Georgia had launched a large-scale military attack against South Ossetia in an attempt to reconquer territory held by the unrecognized government of South Ossetia, which was backed by Russia. Russia responded by advancing into Georgia from South Ossetia, leading to several days of fighting. A preliminary ceasefire was reached on August 12, but on the same day Russian forces shelled the strategically important Georgian town of Gori and later occupied the town for several days.

OPPOSITE: On August 14, Georgian troops began gathering outside the capital Tbilisi, preparing to advance on Gori after the Russians left the town on August 22. On August 28, Russia recognized South Ossetia as an independent republic, but although the region is now governed locally rather than from Tbilisi it is still not recognized as a separate political entity by Georgia.

2008

LEFT: Ricky Berens, Ryan Lochte, and Michael Phelps celebrate as the final member of their team, Peter Vanderkaay, comes in first, winning the men's 4 x 200 meter freestyle relay for the US at the 2008 Olympic Games in Beijing in August. The team's world record of 6:58.56 broke the magical seven-minute barrier and gained Phelps his fifth gold of the games.

OPPOSITE: Phelps in the process of winning his 6th gold of the Beijing Games in the men's 200 meter individual medley, beating the previous world record by 0.57 seconds. He went on to win two more golds, one for the men's 100 meter butterfly and the last for the men's 4 x 100 meter medley relay—breaking Mark Spitz's record of seven golds at the 1972 Munich Olympics, a feat that many had said would be impossible.

2008

ABOVE: A tearful Paula Radcliffe at the end of the women's marathon. Less than three months before the 2008 Olympics the 34-year-old had been diagnosed with a stress fracture of the left femur, and after keeping pace with the leaders for 19 miles she was forced to drop back and then stop. After a brief rest she resumed the race and managed to struggle to the finish in 23rd place.

OPPOSITE: Jamie Staff, Jason Kenny, and Chris Hoy win the gold for Britain in the men's team sprint at Beijing. Hoy emerged as the track's top star, also striking gold in the men's sprint and the men's keirin to become the first Briton in a century to win three golds in one Olympics. In total the British cycling team won seven of a possible ten gold medals on offer across sprint and endurance events in both men's and women's racing.

2008

Christine Ohuruogu of Great Britain
winning the gold in the women's
400 meters at the 2008 Olympic Games
in Beijing on August 19. She became
the first female British athlete to win the
gold in this event, with a time of 49.62
seconds—which was over 2 seconds
slower than the world record. Shericka
Williams of Jamaica took the silver and
Sanya Richards of the United States—
who before the race had been favorite to
win—took the bronze.

Ohuruogu was lucky to be competing,
because in 2006 she had been given
a lifetime ban excluding her from
competing for Britain at future Olympic
Games, after missing three competition
drug tests. She had appealed against the
decision, and the ban was finally lifted in
November 2007.

2008

Sprinter Usain Bolt of Jamaica throws his arms into the air and kisses the ground to celebrate winning the gold and setting a new world record of 19.30 seconds in the men's 200 meters at Beijing. Churandy Martina (Netherlands Antilles) finished second and Wallace Spearmon (US) finished third but both were later disqualified for stepping out of lane, leaving Shawn Crawford and Walter Dix to take silver and bronze respectively for the United States. Bolt had already won a gold in the men's 100 meters, breaking his own world record with a time of 9.69 seconds, and went on to win a third as part of Jamaica's 4 x 100 meters relay team—with the team breaking another world record in the process.

2008

LEFT: Leona Lewis performs at the closing ceremony of the 2008 Olympic Games in Beijing, China on August 24. There were also performances from Led Zeppelin guitarist Jimmy Page, as well as singers from mainland China, Hong Kong, Taiwan, and Singapore. The final ceremony included the Mayor of Beijing, Guo Jinlong, handing over the Olympic flag to the Mayor of London, Boris Johnson, since the next Games were due to be held in 2012 in London.

OPPOSITE: The Russian Prime Minister, Vladimir Putin (center) meets members of the Russian team during his visit to the Olympic village in Beijing. Russia won 23 gold medals, 21 silver and 29 bronze, making a total of 73 and putting them in third place in the medals table behind the US (with 110 medals) and hosts China (with 100 medals).

2008

Scoreboard text:

9.17 · ROLEX

PREVIOUS SETS

4477 R. FEDER
5 8 v
66 R. NADA

ALLE ES RE

ABOVE: Rafael Nadal celebrates his win by climbing into the stands to greet his family. Play was delayed by rain so the match ended over seven hours after it started—with just under five hours spent actually playing—and John McEnroe later described it as "the greatest match I've ever seen." If Federer had won, he would have become the first player to achieve a sixth consecutive Wimbledon singles win since William Renshaw in 1886.

OPPOSITE: Swiss player Roger Federer and Rafael Nadal of Spain pose before the start of the men's singles final at the Wimbledon Tennis Championships on July 6, the third consecutive time they had played each other for the title. Federer (the World No. 1 seed) had won their bouts in the past, but this time he lost to Nadal (No. 2 seed) 6-4, 6-4, 6-7(5), 6-7(8), 9-7, thus breaking his 65-match winning streak on grass.

2008

Corey Webster of the New York Giants breaks up a pass intended for Randy Moss of the New England Patriots on the Patriots' final drive of the game with less then a minute to go. In one of the biggest upsets in Super Bowl history, the Giants won 17–14 over the previously undefeated Patriots. In doing so, the Giants became the first NFC wild card team to win a Super Bowl.

2008

ABOVE: Russian Prime Minister Vladimir Putin out hunting. In May Putin came to the end of his second four-year term as President and under the Russian constitution he could not stay in office for a third consecutive term. However, there was widespread speculation that he might come back for a third term at a later date. During his second term he had instigated a crackdown on media freedom in Russia, which had brought widespread criticism in the West—as well as among liberal Russians.

OPPOSITE: Buildings in ruins after an Israeli air strike in Gaza in December. Israel had received widespread condemnation from countries around the world after carrying out a massive bombing offensive against key targets in the Gaza Strip, which left hundreds dead and injured. The attacks had targeted Hamas government buildings and other symbols of the Islamist group, in the fiercest air offensive in Gaza in decades. In answer to public criticism, Ehud Olmert, Israel's prime minister, said: "Israel wishes to make clear that it will continue to act against terrorist operations and missile fire from the Strip which is intended to harm civilians."

LEFT: Seen here amid celebrations, on July 29 British Foreign Secretary David Miliband had written an article for the *Guardian* newspaper, in which he talked of the Labour Party's future—but did not mention the current Labour leader, Prime Minister Gordon Brown. At the time there was speculation that Brown would have to resign, following a bad Labour defeat at a recent by-election, so Miliband's article was widely seen as a leadership challenge. Although he denied the charge, he did not rule out the possibility that he would run for leadership at some future time.

OPPOSITE: Malik, half-brother of US President-elect Barack Obama, is held aloft by friends and family members at the family's homestead in Kogelo village, Kenya, as they celebrate Obama's historic victory in the US election in November. On hearing the news that Barack Obama had swept to victory and would become America's first black President, Kenyan relatives erupted in cheers singing, "We are going to the White House!"

2008

RIGHT: President Nicolas Sarkozy and his wife, Carla Bruni Sarkozy, attending the commemorations in Verdun to mark the 90th anniversary of the end of the First World War. French and German troops fought for eight months at Verdun during the longest battle of a war that reshaped Europe, and President Sarkozy paid tribute to the millions who died during the four-year conflict. No French or German veterans were in attendance because not one member of the two huge armies that clashed on the fields of Verdun survives, but three of the four surviving British World War I veterans attended a ceremony at the Cenotaph in London. Henry Allingham, 112, Harry Patch, 110, and Bill Stone, 108, represented the Royal Air Force, Army, and Royal Navy respectively.

OPPOSITE: Cristiano Ronaldo of Manchester United receives the Ballon d'Or after being voted the European Footballer of the Year, just before the start of the Champions League group match between Manchester United and Aalborg on December 10 at Old Trafford in Manchester, England.

2008

OPPOSITE: Indian special forces outside the Taj Palace Hotel in Mumbai, which had been targeted by terrorists. More than ten different shooting and bombing incidents occurred during November 26 to 29 across Mumbai, India's largest city, in which nearly 200 people were killed and over 300 injured. The attacks, carried out by members of Lashkar-e-Taiba, an Islamic terrorist organization based in neighboring Pakistan, were widely condemned around the world.

ABOVE: By November 28, all the buildings targeted by terrorists in Mumbai had been taken back by police and security forces, except for the Taj Palace Hotel, which was not secured until the following day. Nine of the terrorists were killed, but one survived and he confirmed that all ten were Pakistani, which caused considerable damage to India's already poor relationship with Pakistan.

On September 7, 2008, James Lockhart, director of the Federal Housing Finance Agency, announced a federal takeover of Fannie Mae and Freddie Mac in "one of the most sweeping government interventions in private financial markets in decades." As of 2008, Fannie Mae and the Federal Home Loan Mortgage Corporation (Freddie Mac) owned or guaranteed about half of the U.S.'s $12 trillion mortgage market. Fannie Mae was established in 1938 as a mechanism to make mortgages more easily available to low-income families.

Heath Ledger as The Joker in the Batman movie, *The Dark Knight*. After he completed filming on the movie Heath Ledger died after accidentally overdosing on prescription drugs, and the film was partly dedicated to his memory. The marketing for the picture before its release include viral messaging, in which emails sent by fans morphed into an image of the Joker. On the film's website a scavenger hunt with hidden messages led to clues in major cities throughout the US, which combined to reveal a new photograph of the Joker and an audio clip of him from the movie saying "And tonight, you're gonna break your one rule." *The Dark Knight* grossed $18.5 million on its first night in the US and is currently the fourth highest-grossing movie of all time.

2009

LEFT: An emotional Kate Winslet accepts her award for Best Performance by an Actress in a Motion Picture—Drama, for her role in *Revolutionary Road* at the 66th annual Golden Globe Awards in Beverly Hills, California, on January 11. Co-star Leonardo di Caprio, won the Best Actor award for his role, and the film also won Best Motion Picture—Drama and Best Director. A claustrophobic account of life in the suburbs, *Revolutionary Road* was well received by the critics and also won three Academy Awards and four BAFTAs later in the year. Winslet also won Best Performance by an Actress in a Supporting Role in a Motion Picture at the Golden Globes for her role in *The Reader*.

OPPOSITE: British director Danny Boyle and actors Freida Pinto and Dev Patel holding the award for Best Motion Picture—Drama for *Slumdog Millionaire* at the Golden Globe Awards. Marketed as "The feel-good film of the decade," *Slumdog Millionaire* tells the story of a child from the slums of Mumbai who wins 20 million rupees on a television game against all the odds, not because he wants the money but to be reunited with his childhood sweetheart. It won three other Golden Globe awards as well as eight Academy Awards and seven BAFTAs.

Israeli soldiers walk towards the northern Gaza Strip in January. Israel army reservists had been thrown into the campaign after a week of heavy air strikes, to try to halt the rocket attacks being made into Israel by Palestinian militants. Israeli troops engaged in heavy clashes with Hamas fighters in northern Gaza, with both sides suffering casualties in the fighting. Israeli Defense Minister Ehud Barak said, "We have carefully weighed all our operations. We are not war-hungry, but we shall not allow a situation in which our towns, villages and civilians are constantly targeted by Hamas." In reply, a spokesman for Palestinian President Mahmoud Abbas condemned the offensive as "a vicious aggression."

Passengers stand on the wings of a US Airways Airbus plane, awaiting rescue after it landed in the Hudson River in New York on January 15. The plane, on a domestic flight with 150 passengers and five crew, had just taken off from LaGuardia Airport but was trying to return after striking a flock of birds, causing damage to the engines. Pilot Chesley Sullenberger, whose skillful splash-landing was credited with saving everyone on board, later testified that a collision with birds certainly caused the disaster. The cockpit windshield "was literally filled with big, dark brown birds," Sullenberger told investigators from the National Transport Safety Board (NTSB).

2009

LEFT: US President Barack Obama delivers his Inaugural Address after being sworn in as the 44th President of the United States in Washington, DC, the first African-American to hold the position. He spoke of the serious challenges facing America, but promised: "Today I say to you that the challenges we face are real. They are serious and they are many. They will not be met easily or in a short span of time. But know this, America—they will be met."

OPPOSITE: On January 20, on the West Front of the Capitol in Washington, Barack H. Obama is sworn in as the 44th President of the United States, as his wife Michelle holds the Bible and their daughters Malia and Sasha look on.

2009

OPPOSITE: President Barack Obama stands alongside his wife, Michelle, with her arm around Jill Biden, wife of Vice-President Joe Biden. Vice-President Biden salutes as former President George W. Bush and his wife, Laura, leave the US Capitol aboard a military helicopter, on the first stage of their journey to their ranch in Crawford, Texas.

RIGHT: President Barack Obama in the Oval Office of the White House on the morning of January 21, the first complete day of his administration. Continuing a White House ritual, Bush had left a note for Obama in his desk in the Oval Office that wished the new President well. As one of his first tasks, Obama telephoned four Middle Eastern leaders—President Hosni Mubarak of Egypt, Prime Minister Ehud Olmert of Israel, King Abdullah of Jordan, and Palestinian leader Mahmoud Abbas—promising his commitment to pursuing Arab-Israeli peace. Later he announced new ethics rules and a pay freeze for White House staff.

2009

ABOVE: From left, Lord Stevenson, Andy Hornby, Sir Fred Goodwin, and Sir Tom McKillop giving evidence to the Treasury Committee at the Houses of Parliament in London on February 10. The four were the former chiefs of the two biggest UK casualties of the banking crisis, Royal Bank of Scotland and HBOS—which both had to be bailed out by the government—and they were now being asked to explain what went wrong.

OPPOSITE: Iranian President Mahmoud Ahmadinejad speaks during a ceremony in Tehran on February 10 marking the 30th anniversary of the 1979 Islamic revolution that toppled the US-backed late Shah Mohammad Reza Pahlavi and brought hard-line clerics to power in Iran. He said that Iran welcomed talks with the new administration of US President Barack Obama on the basis of mutual respect.

Clint Eastwood in action in a scene from *Gran Torino*, in which he starred and also produced and directed. It was his first lead film role for four years; his younger son Scott also had a part, while older son Kyle worked on the musical score. Eastwood plays a Korean War veteran, who is drawn into defending a Hmong family who move in next door.

In February it was announced that US talk-show host Jerry Springer would be making his West End debut as Billy Flynn in the musical *Chicago* at the Cambridge Theatre. "I've a voice for newspapers and a face for radio. When I sing, the audience really get involved because they have to guess where the notes have been," Springer joked as he posed with cast members.

ABOVE: Asylum-seekers in Calais, France, line up for food handouts distributed by local charity workers. Many of them had arrived at the port in the hope of reaching Britain for economic refuge, as jobs throughout Europe vanished because of the credit crunch. The recent release of *Welcome*, a film about a fictional immigrant named Bilal and his story of trying to reach Britain, had prompted French authorities to consider setting up a series of refugee centers.

OPPOSITE: Brazilian Navy divers recovering a large part of the rudder of the Air France A330 aircraft lost in mid-flight over the Atlantic Ocean on June 1. The plane had been on a flight from Brazil to Paris when it suddenly vanished from radar screens after automated messages that indicated numerous failures and warnings. The flight recorder was not recovered so the exact cause of the crash remained a mystery, although there were no signs of explosion or fire. All 228 people on board were killed—the worst loss of life in Air France's 75-year history.

LEFT: Amy Winehouse arriving at Westminster Magistrates Court in London, where she pleaded not guilty to a charge of common assault. The charge related to an incident at a concert the previous September when Winehouse was accused of punching a fan who was trying to take her picture. The judge later decided that any contact may have been accidental and acquitted the troubled singer.

OPPOSITE: British make-up artist Carolyn Roper won first place in the Special Effects Category at the World Bodypainting Festival held in Austria in July. For this photograph she bodypainted six women in seven hours to represent famous songs – from left to right: "Technical Ecstasy" (Black Sabbath), "The Widow" (The Mars Volta), "Wake Up And Smell The Coffee" (The Cranberries), "Absolution" (Muse), "Deceptive Bends" (10cc), and "Audioslave" (Audioslave).

2009

ABOVE: British Prime Minister Gordon Brown welcomes US President Barack Obama and his wife, Michelle, to Downing Street on the President's first official visit to the UK. Mr Brown said of the G20 Summit, "This is an unprecedented financial crisis. People have lost their homes, their jobs, and in some cases, their hope. And President Obama and I are agreed today that the actions we take are global solutions required for global problems."

OPPOSITE: British Foreign Minister David Miliband, US Secretary of State Hilary Clinton, British Prime Minister Gordon Brown, US President Barack Obama, US Treasury Secretary Timothy Geithner and British Chancellor Alastair Darling in the Cabinet Room at Downing Street, London. The President was in London for the 2009 G20 Summit, due to be held in London's ExCel Centre on April 2.

2009

ABOVE: Health workers fumigate against swine flu, a new strain of the H1N1 influenza virus, at a subway station in Mexico City in May. The new virus had first been detected in April in Veracruz, Mexico, and had since spread around the world, with new cases confirmed in Europe and Asia and governments banning flights and preparing quarantines. In June, the outbreak was confirmed as a pandemic and by the end of December there had been nearly 10,000 deaths worldwide.

OPPOSITE: Displaced Tamils from the north of Sri Lanka make their way from the no-fire zone, after Sri Lankan Army troops gained control of the area of Puthukkudiyirippu in April, pushing the Tamil Tigers into the zone, which was set up for civilians. On May 16, Sri Lankan President Mahindi Rajapaksa declared victory over the Tamil Tigers, bringing to an end the long-running civil war. For over 25 years, the conflict had brought hardship to the people of Sri Lanka, as well as damaging the environment.

2009

RIGHT: To publicize the opening of the new musical, *Sister Act*, in London's West End in May, several "nuns" abseil down the outside of the London Palladium. The musical was based on the smash-hit movie of 1992, which starred Whoopi Goldberg and Maggie Smith, but the lead character was changed from a Las Vegas singer to a disco diva, and featured a new score by eight-time Oscar winner Alan Menken.

OPPOSITE: Zachary Quinto as Spock and Chris Pine as Captain James T. Kirk in the new movie of *Star Trek*, the eleventh to be based on the franchise. It told the story of Spock and Kirk before they joined the USS *Enterprise*, and recounted their subsequent battle against an enemy from the future. The film aimed to be faithful to the original *Star Trek* series, but the time-traveling storyline allowed considerable license in continuity. It was very highly praised by the critics and became the tenth-highest grossing film of 2009.

RIGHT: Prince Harry thrills pupils at a New York community center by taking part in an energetic obstacle course during his first official state visit overseas. The 24-year-old member of the British royal family joined in with youngsters to enjoy the obstacle course at Harlem Children's Zone, which works with 8,000 disadvantaged children.

OPPOSITE: In May Astronaut Andrew Feustel, STS-125 Mission Specialist, and Astronaut John Grunsfeld carried out vital maintenance work on the Hubble Space Telescope in space, including installing new battery packs that will allow it to function until at least 2014.

2009

The 2009 British Grand Prix, held at Silverstone on June 21, was won by German driver Sebastian Vettel with British driver and championship leader Jenson Button finishing in sixth place. This was the last year that the race was due to be held at Silverstone—the following year it was to be held at Donington, but in November the new venue revealed that it had failed to secure financing to upgrade its facilities. For several weeks the whole future of British Grand Prix racing hung in the balance, but in December Silverstone announced that they had signed a 17-year deal to host the British Grand Prix from 2010, ensuring the race was not dropped from the calendar.

2009

OPPOSITE: "The Boss" Bruce Springsteen performs with the E Street Band at the Glastonbury Festival, in Somerset, England, in June. Springsteen powered through a set that—at nearly three hours long—was way past his allotted time span, but nobody dared to pull the plug. At one point he was joined by the singer from Gaslight Anthem for "No Surrender," and during the encore he played "Hard Times," a folk song from 1855, delivered with a sense of defiance.

RIGHT: Performing on the Pyramid Stage at Glastonbury, Neil Young kicked off with a hammering version of "Hey Hey My My (Into the Black)," before plunging straight into "Mansion on the Hill."

2009

OPPOSITE: Lady Gaga brightens up the Other Stage at Glastonbury. Late on Friday night, in Club Dada, she also did a riotous secret gig. At first the weather was bright and sunny, but soon the sky clouded over and Glastonbury's signature rainstorms ensued, leading to the usual muddy conditions underfoot. For once the bad weather didn't last very long, and festivalgoers refused to have their spirits dampened.

RIGHT: Lily Allen performs wearing one white glove in a silent tribute to Michael Jackson. The previous evening news of his untimely death had swept through the crowd and there were many tributes celebrating his music throughout the weekend.

2009

OPPOSITE: Coordinating festivalgoers at the Glastonbury Festival, the largest greenfield music and performing arts festival in the world. Tickets for the 2009 Festival sold out eight weeks beforehand, and by June 24 a record 90,396 people had already set up camp on Worthy Farm's rolling hills. There were 134,000 tickets sold for the weekend, plus a further 6,000 for Sunday. It was a far cry from the first festival in 1970, which only 1,500 had attended, at a ticket price of only £1 including free milk.

LEFT: Fergie from the Black Eyed Peas appears in an eye-catching cut-out playsuit and high heels.

2009

LEFT: One of Michael Jackson's last public appearances. On June 25, news came that superstar Michael Jackson had collapsed and died in Los Angeles, where he was rehearsing for a series of major comeback concerts, entitled This Is It. The concerts were due to begin on July 13 and tickets had already sold out. Jackson had indicated that they were his "final curtain call" and that afterwards he would retire from performing.

OPPOSITE: The Jackson brothers (from left to right in yellow ties) Randy, Marlon, Jackie, Jermaine, and Tito, accompany the casket at the Michael Jackson public memorial service held at Staples Center in Los Angeles on July 7. Several major stars performed at the service, which was watched by an estimated 31.1 million people across America. Jackson was not buried until September 3, when he was laid to rest at Forest Lawn Memorial Park in Glendale, California.

2009

ABOVE: The Boston Red Sox and Chicago White Sox stand in silence before the game on August 26 at Fenway Park, Boston, to honor the late Edward Kennedy. The Massachusetts senator had died earlier that day after a battle with brain cancer. Kennedy was involved in the Chappaquiddick incident in 1969, in which a young woman died after a car he was driving went off a bridge into deep water, but by 2009 was considered as a senior statesman and major liberal influence in the senate.

OPPOSITE: British player Andy Murray after winning 2–6, 6–3, 6–3, 5–7, 6–3 over the Swiss Stanislas Wawrinka on June 29, thus taking his place in the quarter-finals of the Wimbledon Tennis Championship. The match did not finish until after 10.30 p.m.—the latest finish at Wimbledon ever—and it also made history by being the first men's singles match and the first full match to be played with the new Centre Court roof closed.

2009

ABOVE: England's Ian Bell in action on the first day of the four-day England v Australia Fifth Test match, at the Oval in London on August 20. He scored 72, laying a foundation

2009

LEFT: A protester against the Iraq war sets fire to a plastic mask of former British Prime Minister Tony Blair at the start of the second week of the Iraq Inquiry, chaired by Sir John Chilcot. The public hearings began on November 24 and will run until February 2010, taking evidence from those with first-hand experience of the development and implementation of British government policy in Iraq.

OPPOSITE: The towering 327-feet-tall Ares I-X rocket moves toward launch pad 39B at NASA's Kennedy Space Center in Cape Canaveral, Florida on October 20. The rocket was launched for an unmanned two-minute powered test flight on October 28, designed to provide NASA with an enormous amount of data to be used to improve the design and safety of the next generation of American spaceflight vehicles, which could again take humans beyond low Earth orbit.

2009

US President Barack Obama speaks during a plenary session at the Bella Center in Copenhagen on December 18, 2009 on the 12th day of the COP15 UN Climate Change Conference. The Copenhagen Accord was drafted by the US, China, India, Brazil and South Africa on December 18, and judged a "meaningful agreement" by the United States government. It was "recognised", but not "agreed upon", in a debate of all the participating countries the next day, and it was not passed unanimously. The document recognised that climate change is one of the greatest challenges of the present and that actions should be taken to keep any temperature increases to below 2°C. President Obama said that the agreement would need to be built on in the future and that "We've come a long way but we have much further to go."

ACKNOWLEDGMENTS

Written and edited by:
Tim Hill; Gareth Thomas; Murray Mahon; Marie Clayton; Duncan Hill; Jane Benn; Alison Gauntlett; Alice Hill

****

The photographs in this book are from the archives of the Daily Mail. Thanks to all the photographers who have contributed and the film and television companies who have provided Associated Newspapers with promotional stills.
Every effort has been made to correctly credit photographs provided. In case of inaccuracies or errors we will be happy to correct them in future printings of this book.

Thanks to all the staff at Associated Newspapers who have made this book possible.
Particular thanks to Alan Pinnock.
Thanks also to Steve Torrington, Dave Sheppard and Brian Jackson.

Thanks to the many photographers who have contributed including: Jamie Wiseman, Alex Lentati, Jeremy Selwyn, Roland Hoskins, Andy Hooper, Cavan Pawson, Glenn Copus, Craig Hibbert, Krestine Havemann, Denis Jones, Murray Sanders, Mark Large, Ian McIlgorm, Ken Towner, David Crump, Colin Davey, Mike Forster, Nigel Howard, Giles Keyte, Alan Walter, Brian Bould, Jeff Morris, Graham Hughes, Mark Lloyd, Paul Lewis, Sue Adler, Nick Holt, Keith Waldegrave, Mark Richards, Michael Thomas, David O'Neill, Graham Chadwick, Nasser Nasser, Tim Wimborne, Malcolm Clarke, Michael Dunlea,, J. Scott Applewhite, Lynn Hilton, Leonhard Foeger, Bruce Adams, Oka Budhi, Mike Floyd, Rob McMillan, Peter Jordan, Jaime Razuri, Nick Skinner, Steve Waters, Adam Elder, Jamal Saidi, Mahmoud Tawil, Nick Cornish, Graham Jepson, Terry Bradford, Oliver Lim, Max Nash, David J. Phillip, Brian Snyder, David Parker, Tony Buckingham, Barry Phillips, Burhan Ozbilici, Graham Hussey, John Cogill, Joe Dunne, Plinio Lepri, Michael Chester, Howard Walker, Graham Hughes, Matt Writtle, Michael Chester, George Jaworskyj, Jenny Goodall, Nigel Howard, Ian Hodgson, Keith Waldegrave
With contributions from photographers: Manuel Balce Ceneta, Plinio Lepri, Gerald Herbert, Chris Bacon, Marko Djurica, Steve Parsons, Dmitry Astakhov, Matt Dunham, Mohammed Salem, Paul Buck, Brendan McDermid, Pat Benic, Saul Loeb, Hasan Sarbakhshian, Rodrigo Abd, Romano-Arturo Mari, Claudio Onorati, Neil Cohen, Chuck Kennedy, Ho, Pete Souza.

Additonal photographs courtesy Getty Images

Al Messerschmidt/Getty Images 88-89, Al Bello/Getty Images 198-199, Andrew D. Bernstein/ Getty Images 234-235, Scott Boehm/Getty Images 252-253, Lisa Blumenfeld/Getty Images 290-291, Doug Pensinger/Getty Images 328-329, Asif Hassan, /AFP/Getty Images 278, Kevork Djansezian/Getty Images 373, Elsa/Getty Images 375

Courtesy Nasa

138,258,363,379

Film and Television:

Castaway, Universal Pictures 8, Gladiator, Universal Studios/Dreamworks 9, Billy Elliot, Universal Focus 22, Bridget Jones's Diary, Mirimax Films/Universal Pictures 50, Moulin Rouge, Twentieth Century Fox 60, Lord of the Rings, New Line Cinema 51, Spiderman, Columbia Pictures 123, Men in Black 2, Columbia Pictures 124, The Bourne Identity, Universal Studios 125, Shaun of the Dead, Universal Studios, Oliver Upton 177, Troy, Warner Bros. 176, Million Dollar Baby, Warner Bros 208, X-Men The Last Stand, Twentieth Century Fox, Kerry Hayes 260, The History Boys, Fox Searchlight 271, Casino Royale, Metro-Goldwyn-Mayer/Columbia Pictures/EON Productions/United Artists/ Sony pictures 270, Atonement, Alex Bailey/Focus Features/Universal Pictures/StudioCanal 286, No Country For Old Men, AP Photo/Miramax Films, Richard Foreman) 287, The Dark Knight, Warner Bros. 339, Gran Torino, Warner Bros. 350, Star Trek, Paramount Pictures 360

Published by Transatlantic Press
First published in 2010

Transatlantic Press
38 Copthorne Road
Croxley Green, Hertfordshire
WD3 4AQ

© Atlantic Publishing
For photograph copyrights see pages 382–3

All rights reserved. No part of this publication may be reproduced, stored in a retrieval system, or transmitted,
in any form or by any means, without the prior written permission of the copyright holder.

A catalogue record for this book is available from the British Library.

ISBN 978-1-907176-11-1

Printed in China